Dare to Break Bread

Eucharist in Desert and City

Geoffrey Howard

Foreword by Bishop Trevor
Huddleston

Dare to Break Bread

Geoffrey Howard

Pendlebury Press Ltd 20 May Road, Pendlebury, Manchester M27 5FR   2017

Available only from Amazon ISBN 9781520163376

First Published in 1992 in paperback by Darton, Longman and Todd Limited

A catalogue record for this book is available from the British Library

Contents

TO THE SPIRITUAL FAMILY OF
CHARLES DE FOUCAULD

Preface

These meditations present challenges and dilemmas that face all who break bread in our Lord's name. I am grateful to the people of my former parish and neighbourhood for allowing me to tell their stories.

Though I use an Anglican rite in this book, the components included appear in Eucharists of most Christian traditions. The meditations follow the chronology of the liturgy except where events related in them have a chronology of their own. For example, the meditation on the creed is deliberately placed late.

Foreword

Sometimes, I find myself longing for at least a five-year moratorium on all books about Christian spirituality. It has become virtually impossible to read so many. Moreover, any serious attempt to do so leads to the conclusion that a great number of them are platitudinous and repetitive and lead not to inspiration, but to inertia. Therefore it is, for me at least, a small miracle (but truly a miracle) to read this book and to find that instant frisson of empathy on virtually every page.

I have to confess that my reactions to Geoffrey Howard's theme are conditioned by a shared devotion (if that is a permissible word) to Charles de Foucauld. For me that devotion began when, as an undergraduate at Oxford in the early thirties I read Rene Bazin's biography of that extraordinary French soldier, explorer and hermit. A missionary who never converted a single one of the tribe (the Tuareg of the Sahara) to whom he dedicated his life. A contemplative for whom the strictest Cistercian way of life was never strict enough. A priest who, for most of the time he was in the desert, had to celebrate the

Eucharist (with special dispensation) in solitude. A deeply patriotic Frenchman whose patriotism was entirely subsumed in his commitment, in that tiny space of desert stones and sand, to the whole of God's world. A mystic whose dedication to the Blessed Sacrament was so absolute as to exclude the need for any other object or sign or symbol of worship. Geoffrey Howard has succeeded in making the connection perfectly between this unbelievably austere spirituality and all the complex needs of the Christian community struggling to find a meaning for "mission' in the desert of our Western secularist society.

I wish everyone involved in the Decade of Evangelism could be compelled to read this book before presiding over committee meetings or preaching sermons. Evangelism is not about preaching the gospel but about living it. This is indeed a small book, but "small is beautiful' and, in the case of this book, life-saving as well.

+ TREVOR HUDDLESTON CR

Introduction: The Road to Assékrem

I am on Mount Assékrem, 9000 feet above sea level, in the middle of the Sahara Desert. The mountain drops away almost sheer at my feet into a broad, dusty valley. Beyond the valley is a panorama of eroded, extinct volcanoes and grey basalt towers. It's more like the moon than the earth. At my heels is the summit, a plateau of two square miles, covered with loose blackened rocks which clatter like dinner plates when you walk over them. In every direction there is dust and rock.

In 1911, Charles de Foucauld, a former army officer and explorer, by then ordained priest, came here to live as a hermit. There was barely another Christian between him and Algiers 1,200 miles away. Up to his death at the hands of rebels in 1916, he had few followers. Since then, the fraternity about which he wrote and dreamt has come into being. The Little Brothers and Sisters of Jesus live in a number of houses and hermitages across Europe and North Africa. They have built five hermitages here on Assékrem, each one a distance from the rest, spaced round the rim of the plateau. Only two are permanently occupied, the other hermitages being used by visitors.

Charles de Foucauld lived here alone. His chief contact with humanity was with the nomadic Tuareg, not one of whom, during his lifetime or since, is said to have become Christian. Though he had infrequent contact with other Christians, his passion for the Eucharist, the most communal of all acts of worship, was stronger than any I have heard of or read about. Yet, paradoxically, he chose to live where he would rarely share bread and wine with others. It is to this same desert place that I have come to contemplate the challenges which the Eucharist presents to the Christian community. I am putting on Eucharistic spectacles and viewing disparate events of my past from this extraordinary vantage point. Not every meditation will draw directly on my experience here. This hermitage is the location of meditation, but will not always be the subject of it.

Getting here has been a long pilgrimage. I passed within twenty miles of here in 1975 when I crossed the Sahara on foot. My mind was too full of other things for me to make a detour, something I have always regretted. This time, I have come in my Transit van – 1000 miles to Marseilles, a ferry to Algiers and a 1,200 mile drive due south to the mountain town of Tamanrasset. From there, the 50 miles and the further 4500 feet climb took eight hours without a break. It was the toughest track I've ever encountered, steep enough to stall my van when I had it in first gear with my foot to the floor. At other times, I had to manoeuvre boulders out of the way or use them to fill up gullies that were otherwise impassable.

For a few days, I am void of human contact, living in a vacant hermitage. I am praying and collecting my thoughts in preparation for writing this book. What better than a place of stones to contemplate bread? What better than a waterless place to contemplate wine? From here I go for a holiday to the Dordogne in France where bread and wine abound. From there I return to finish the book in Salford where bread is hard earned and where wine means sherry drunk at Christmas.

At the time of writing this introduction, the meditations are hardly begun. It is my prayer that I will write them for those who, like me, usually leave their experience of the Eucharist locked in church. What is the challenge of the Eucharist after you've received a handshake at the church door and gone to Sunday lunch? We will see the Eucharist not just as a sacrament of a dead Christ on a cross, but of a living Christ in the world. Come now, meet a few of my friends and dare to share with us bread and wine.

GEOFFREY HOWARD
ASSÉKREM

1. Expectations

The Lord be with you.

The wheels spin, flinging up dust and stones in an attempt not to slip back. The engine stalls. I restart with massive revs, letting in the gear and smelling the clutch burning. The last half mile to Assékrem takes twenty minutes. I park 200 feet below the summit and climb with a loaded rucksack towards a stone shack perched above me on the edge of the plateau. Alain, the only Little Brother in residence, stands outside it, watching me. As I arrive, he smiles, welcoming me. We look back down at the vehicle track. It plummets between lesser peaks and is swallowed up in a gorge.

Alain gives me a cup of coffee on his patio - a rocky ledge covered by a wooden shade. He then escorts me from his hermitage across the plateau. For twenty-five minutes, we clatter over broken rock. When we reach the distant edge, my dry-stone hermitage is twenty yards down the slope, almost invisible against the mountain side. We scramble down and open the wooden door. Opposite the doorway is a mattress on a stone slab. To the left is a tiny kitchen with a camping stove and a plastic bowl. There's a table to my right. Everything apart from the mattress is dilapidated and covered in dust.

Alain demonstrates how to use the stove, but discovers that the gas bottle is almost empty and the gas pipe split. I do not mind - I have brought a portable stove and gas lamp. We shake hands and he leaves. I root around the place to discover its secrets. There is a candle lantern, but no candles, three broken oil lamps and no oil. A mirror, cracked three ways, is hanging on a nail. Below it, on a shelf, is a red enamel teapot, a pan with its handle wired on, and a cigarette lighter which needs refilling. Next to them, matches, string and nails are kept in old tins. On other ledges, there are clothes pegs, a mousetrap, toilet paper, a Bible; a Madonna painted on slate and a copy of the rule of the Little Brothers of Jesus. On the floor, is a dustpan made from a tin can. There is an adequate supply of cutlery and crockery. Two hundred litres of water are stacked around the walls in large plastic containers. Tea towels and blankets hang from a rope stretched across the ceiling. Everything is old, worn and covered in dust, but otherwise serviceable. But for the food on the shelves, I would guess that the place has not been occupied since the 1930s. There are exotic teas which look like recent acquisitions. The Ovaltine and milk powder should have been consumed by 1988 according to the labels. The packet soups and biscuits look twenty years old. It is hard to tell how long the rice, macaroni and coffee have been here.

I look at the stone walls, the utensils and feel at home. It is the end of a long pilgrimage, but I have only a vague idea how to use my time. I'm used to prayer in small doses, not for days on end. I expected that, having got here, I would have been swept along by the spirit of the place, but my senses are aware of little other than what I can see.

I sit on the only chair, say the office and pray for a while but after an hour, I'm feeling like a break. I then read through the liturgy of the Eucharist but can't settle. I get up, dampen a cloth and wipe down every container and surface apart from the stone walls.

Now that the place is clean, I sit down and ask myself what I am expecting here. If I could be guaranteed an immediate answer to prayer, what would I pray? This is not just a question for here. I have asked it many times, not least when I pray in preparation for the Eucharist. This is then where I begin. I ask myself what to expect from the Eucharist.

9.15 on a Sunday morning, I put on my cassock, leave the house and walk the 300 yards to church. Folk at the door are giving out books. A few people are already in the pews. Some are whispering, others praying.

I go into the side chapel to pray. I am expecting to be uplifted during the Eucharist. I tell God that I want to feel his presence, but what I dare not admit is that I want to feel good. In order to achieve this, I have carefully chosen the hymns and prepared the sermon. I believe that if God doesn't 'warm my heart', I will not have met him at all. In my prayers, I tell him that this is what I expect. "Lord, I am full of hope and joy. I know you will bless me with the knowledge of your presence."

An elderly Nigerian goes into his mud-brick house, takes a stand-up bath using a bucket and puts on clean clothes. He packs a few belongings into an old flour sack, says goodbye to his wife and follows a path between fields of millet stubble. He walks a mile across the bush to a road junction to wait for a lift. An hour or two later, I am dropped off by a lorry next to him. We introduce ourselves, tell each other where we are from and to where we are going and then we stand and wait.

It is early April, just before the rains. Scorched savannah stretches as far as the eye can see, under a cloudless sky. Now and then I look at the old man in his clean, patched-up robe and the flour sack by his side. In one hour, two vehicles pass.

Leaves blow across the road. I am waiting for God to bless me with a lift. The sun beats down, but I am content. I am assured of my father's love. I will wait for him no matter how long it takes. A car passes, the sun beats down and more leaves scuttle across the road. I am sure that God will bless me.

Robert is one of my parishioners, single and in his early thirties. He is walking back from my home in Salford, approaching his block of flats. The doors at the entrance have been ripped from their hinges and the glass smashed. He climbs up the communal stairway in the dark. Vandals have torn out the light fittings. The handrail has been pulled off the concrete wall. Most of the tenants have moved out and their flats are boarded up. On the stairs, he pushes past huddled shapes and the red points of lighted cigarettes. There is the smell of cannabis and stale urine.

He enters his third floor home and sinks into an arm chair. His mother is on the settee from which she rarely moves. Their flat has no lift; she can hardly walk and is almost blind. Robert's sister is next to her. She suffers from schizophrenia and is always sedated. His elderly father is watching television. They are a Christian family - mother, in particular, enjoys having the Bible read to her. The family sits in the same chairs from morning to night, year in, year out, waiting for God to bless them with better health and with a council house. Robert is not indolent. He keeps himself and his clothes spotless. He has fought hard to hold down jobs, but his medical condition always grinds him down.

Robert is the only member of his family with much mobility, but he suffers from anxiety attacks and depression. He has a faith in God but is usually too depressed to enjoy it. He has been treated by many doctors and I have prayed with him regularly over many years. At his request, I and others have found him places in therapeutic communities up and down the country. In each case, temporary relief is followed by more depression. Men and women with gifts of counselling and healing have seen him. He has exhausted and depressed himself seeking medical and Christian help.

With his parents and sister, he sits and waits for God to bless them with healing and with a new home. They want to be free from physical and mental torment and they would like a house with a garden. Year in, year out, they wait. Friends pray for them and now and then take them to be prayed for by those with specialist ministries.

9.30 Sunday morning, I am still in the side chapel, waiting for the Eucharist. I know that Robert will not be with us today. When he sees others enjoying the presence of God, he feels like a hungry person with no money looking through a restaurant window. When he comes to church, he usually walks out before the end. The happier others are, the more depressed he is. Usually, instead of coming to church, he sits at home and waits, as he has done for fifteen years.

I, too, am waiting for God to bless me, not with a new home and better health but with the knowledge of his presence. Though I dare not admit it to myself, all I want is the right kind of feelings. I don't want God's presence, but the *thrill* of his presence. I tell myself I want to hear his voice but what I really want is to be filled with sweet feelings. I pray "Let me know your presence", but really mean, "Lord, let my emotions be touched".

And so I pray, "Lord, I'm expecting you to reveal yourself. At the moment, I only hear the rustle of clothing, whispers from the pews, the cry of a baby, but when the Eucharist begins, you will touch me with your presence. I do not know when you will touch me nor how, but I am confident, full of joy."

I take off my denim cap and run fingers through my soaked hair. The African has been motionless and expressionless. I wonder what is so fragile in his sack that he will not sit on it. He is an old man. He must be tired but he looks more patient than I am, more resigned to waiting.

I can only hear the wind blowing leaves. The sun beats down. I am content. I am assured of my father's love. I will wait for him no matter how long it takes. He will bless me with a lift. A car passes, the sun beats down and I wait.

One spring morning the doorbell rings. I get up from my desk and find William, a homeless alcoholic, on the step. He wants something to eat. He sits in my porch while I make him a sandwich and a cup of tea. A few days later, he returns, asking me to find him somewhere to stay. He sits in my porch while I make calls on his behalf. The first three hostels that I telephone know him and won't have him. I am relieved when the fourth one agrees to take him.

Weeks later, he is back in my porch, having been evicted from the hostel for fighting. I make two unsuccessful phone calls for him, but have to abandon the attempt to go to a meeting. I return three hours later and he's still in my porch. Nine o'clock that night, when I have almost given up, I am successful and drive him to his new accommodation. While he's in my van, he says, "At my time of life, I need a place of my own. I've been in and out of hostels for twenty years. I'm getting weary."

It is 1966. With fifteen other undergraduates, I am engaged in a student mission to a parish in Swindon. I busy myself with house-groups and meetings, trying to share the love of Christ. It is not easy to keep my mind on the mission. For two of us, David and myself, the results of our first-year resits are due. We failed in June and resat in August. A year of sleeping during the day and socialising at night has taken its toll. Failure this time will mean returning home and, for me, puts an obstacle in the way of ordination. In my case, graduation has been made a prerequisite of theological training. I am worried and do much praying. Whenever I get the chance, I talk with David about the possibility of failure. I have no contingency plans. Before we leave Swindon, we will know the results. Our tutor will receive them by telephone.

The day the results are published has arrived. We are in the church hall waiting for a meeting to begin. Our tutor is outside on the telephone. Any moment he will enter the room with our results. My stomach is churning. My parents were proud - the first member of our large extended family to get to university. How can I face them with failure? What will I do? I think of the time I should have spent studying - days on the river or in bed and nights playing cards.

The church hall is filling with people. I look at my watch many times in the space of five minutes. I am sitting next to one of the locals, a cheerful man with a bald head. My worried face is set in stiff plastic, unable to smile. "Lord, you know I am waiting for you to bless me with favourable results." David is across the room. He looks worried. He has parents, too.

I can hear only the wind blowing leaves across the hot tarmac. I am expecting God to bless me with a lift. Silence and waiting. The sun beats down. I am content to wait. I am assured of my father's love. I will wait for him no matter how long it takes. A car passes, the sun beats down and I wait, expectantly. A car appears in the distance. It is slowing down. It is going to stop. It passes the African and draws up to me. It is a new Mercedes, black and shiny, driven by a man in his thirties. On the back seat are his two wives. He opens the passenger door and invites me to get in. "No", I say, pointing to the man with the flour sack. "Give him the lift. He was here first." The man with the flour sack turns and looks but stays where he is. His face is beaded with sweat. "Give the old man the lift. He's been here for hours."

"I am offering you a lift, not him."

"Please take him."

"I want you to get in, not him."

At least if I get in now, it will be easier for the man with the flour sack when the next car comes. If I refuse this blessing, neither of us will be blessed. If l receive this blessing, then it will be better for the other man when the next car comes. Better still, I should intercede for the old man. He is tired and hasn't the opportunity to speak up for himself.

"If you don't get in, I drive away."

I am in the side chapel, waiting on God in prayer. I am content, full of joy. At the moment, I hear only the rustle of clothing, whispers, the cry of a baby, but when the Eucharist begins, he will thrill me with his presence.

"Geoff, Elijah had expectations like yours. He was full of zeal, waiting for me to speak to him on the mountain."

"You're going to remind me that there was a strong wind, an earthquake and a fire but that you chose to reveal yourself in the breeze."

"Your love of wind, earthquake and fire means that you usually miss me. But, like last week, you can have what you pray for."

"Yes, you answered my prayer last week. As the Gospel was read, I heard your voice. My heart flooded with the knowledge of your presence. Your love overwhelmed me. Later, as we sang, it was as if you were seated high above the altar in your ascended glory. Then, as I received the sacrament, I knew that I was in you and you in me. You had touched my heart. It was as if my feet were off the ground."

"You always expect to be on cloud nine in worship, don't you? If I don't heal you or bless you with feelings that put an inane grin on your face, you feel that the worship is dead. It's fine for you. You have high hopes when you come to the Eucharist, but what about Frank? He turned up last week for the first time in years because his wife had died. He came without his glasses and couldn't follow the service. He couldn't share your souped-up feelings. Does that mean that I was not with him? And what about Jane with her two little boys? She was so distracted by them that she didn't even hear the Gospel, let alone get *blessed* by it. Was I any less close to her than I was to you? And do you remember what happened when you went home after the Eucharist? Robert had walked over from that awful block of flats and was waiting to see you. He said to you, 'When you turn to God, who else can you turn to? I turned to him and he pushed me and my family aside. I have waited for years for God to bless me. I'm still waiting. I feel suicidal.' So how did you reply?"

"Everything I might have said about your love, I had said before. I had used up my vocabulary. I had done everything I could and still he was no better. I was speechless."

"You didn't dare tell him that you had been on cloud nine in the Eucharist. He was still waiting for me to bless him with a few of the basics that you take for granted. Knowing my presence is more than titillation. It is more than being on a high. If you want that kind of experience, I'll send you tickets for the cup final."

The African in the Mercedes repeats, "If you don't get in, I drive away."

At least if I get in now, it will be easier for the man with the flour sack when the next car comes. If I refuse this blessing, neither of us will be blessed. If I receive this blessing, then it will be better for the other man later.

I get in the car, thanking God. What a wonderful God we have. He has been faithful. He has kept his promise and, blessed me with a lift. We drive off. I try not to think of the old man with the flour sack still waiting under the sun.

William, the alcoholic has been evicted again and is back in my porch. I am in and out of the house all day, carrying out parochial duties. Each time I return home, I make unsuccessful phone calls for him. In the evening, I go out again, leaving him in my porch. When I return, he's gone. I bump into him a few days later on the street. He is sleeping in derelict buildings. "I've been looking for a place of my own for years", he says. "Please help me."

"I'm on my way to a meeting', I say. "Call around at tea time." By the time I go to bed, he still hasn't called round. I wonder where he has found to put his head.

Back on the student mission, the meeting is about to begin. Our tutor is in the parish office in the same building. He puts down the phone, having ascertained our examination results. He walks into the meeting room, catches my eye and smiles. He is behind David, looking over at me. He mouths at me. "Congratulations!' The waiting is over. God has been faithful. The tutor puts his hand on David's shoulder and whispers in his ear. They leave the room looking grave and I know that David will not be with us next term.

I am still in the side chapel, asking God to meet me in the Eucharist. "Aren't you sick of blessings", he asks, "like children on Easter morning who eat all their chocolate eggs at once? When you expect titillation, what are you saying about your relationship with me? Isn't my quiet presence enough? And while you are expecting me to make you feel good, what about the others? How about Dave? How did he feel about your exam success? How about the man with the flour sack? Have you any idea what happened to him that day? How about Robert, not to mention Frank? You are like a poor man who inherits a fortune, keeps it to himself, and expects his starving friends to be happy for him.

"Your children have bikes and when they want newer and better bikes, you say, "There are children who have no bikes. Be content with what you have. You are like a child always asking for toys. Why do you always want blessings? Sometimes you go into your children's bedroom when they are asleep. You touch them, bless them and pray for them. They receive a blessing, but never know it. In the morning when they are squabbling over who has eaten the last of the favourite breakfast cereal, you and I are aware of the blessing they have received. The fact that they don't know about it doesn't diminish its power."

"Lord, as I come to the Eucharist today, I want your touch to be like that given to a sleeping child. You can give the wind, fire and earthquake to those who need it. Let your presence be like that of the desert breeze."

2. Confession

Almighty God, our heavenly Father, we have sinned against you and against our fellow men

5.30 a.m. I wake, light a match, switch on the gas lamp and put on my track suit against the dawn air. When I've made a cup of tea, I take it outside with my Bible and prayer book to watch the dawn. I sit on a huge chair shaped like a throne. It is built of stone, looking out from the mountain side over the valley. The tops of the distant monoliths are tinged with the gold of the early sun. The valleys remain deep grey. I stay here for prayers. As I make my confession and find absolution, my thoughts turn to those who find it hard to receive forgiveness.

At home, I face the congregation and say, "Let us confess our sins to almighty God'. I kneel and join in the words with them. It is a personal moment between me and God. When I have made my confession with the congregation, I stand, facing them and pronounce the absolution. It should be a glorious moment: God is giving pardon to the penitent. Too often, the pardon is not received. God sends a cheque which is not cashed.

In 1969, my wife and I were tutors at a teachers' training college in Nigeria. Eighteen-year-old Elijah cooked, shopped and washed for us. We said we would never have a servant, but he came with the job. The day we arrived, he was waiting for us. I told him I didn't want him, but he pleaded. He needed work. It turned out best for us, too. Housework was labour intensive. There was no running water and no gas. To make a cup of tea, wood had to be found to burn in the stove. To press our clothes, we had to light a fire to make hot charcoal to put in the iron.

We wanted to break the stereotypical model of servant and master. When we first met him, we asked him to sit down. He sat on the floor and could never be persuaded to use our chairs. We invited him to eat with us but he never so much as took a cup of water in our presence.

He worked five hours in the mornings and three in the evening. In the afternoons, he was free, but before he went home, while the fire was still alight, he put water in a Thermos flask for the afternoon tea. He was good at his job and always ready to raise a smile. When I asked him to go to the market, he replied, "I can't go. I'm dirty. Look", he said, pointing at his legs, "I'm a disgrace. I'm white!" His legs had been lightened by wood ash.

After five months, he became less cheerful and was often late in the mornings. Then there was a hole burnt in my best shirt and strange scratches on the cutlery.

He was never around at four o'clock when we came back from lessons, but the flask of hot water was. We'd make three cups of tea, take three doughnuts out of the tin and sit under the veranda with Paul. He was a local ten-year-old, who, in exchange for afternoon tea and three pence, spent a few minutes teaching us to speak Hausa. He was in our home much of his free time and, unlike Elijah, was happy to eat with us.

One afternoon, as we were settled with our note books, I opened the tin expecting to find five doughnuts but found only three. It didn't matter. There was still one each. We got on with the Hausa lesson, but I was puzzled why Elijah had become dishonest and unreliable. Then, one evening when guests were due for dinner, we discovered that the fire was out and no food prepared. Elijah had disappeared, never to return. His brother told us next day that he had joined the army. He had felt that his resignation would have insulted us. Better, he thought, that we should sack him. He had therefore done his job deliberately badly. In his eyes, leaving us was the breaking of a relationship. Damaging our belongings was a lesser evil than saying, "I no longer wish to be in a close relationship with you." In his mind, it would have been better for us, rather than him, to have caused the rift.

From the day he left, we heard nothing of Elijah but, twelve years after returning to England, we received a letter from Paul who had taught us Hausa. It began, "I don't know if you remember me". He went on to say how close we had been and how, in a small way, my wife and I had been like a mother and

21

father to him. Then he wrote, "I beg your forgiveness. For twelve years, I have wept over my guilt. I stole two doughnuts from you." He went on to ask us not to be angry with him.

How could I be angry? He imagined that I would see dishonesty. I saw only the courage of one who would risk his reputation rather than live a lie. I put a reply in the next post. Three weeks later, a second letter came. He told us how unspeakably happy he was. The burden of guilt that had crushed him for years had gone. He added that it had been guilt that had prevented him from writing to us. Now that the guilt was gone, our relationship was renewed. Confession and forgiveness had brought us together.

Harry, like Zacchaeus, was a little man. Not a collector of taxes but of rents. He was a familiar sight in the streets of our city, in his trilby and tweed overcoat, rent book under his arm and pipe in his mouth. There was no fear of this rent man. When families couldn't pay, there was always an understanding ear and word of consolation. When their poverty depressed them, he tried to raise a smile. "You think you've got worries', he'd say. "It's no joke getting money out of people when you're my size. It's not that I'm too short to be a policeman that worries me. It's that I'm not tall enough to be a policewoman, either." He had an impish grin and a twinkle in his eye. Yet, when he walked up my path one summer morning, the sparkle had gone.

I led him into my study and we sat facing each other in arm chairs. He tried to speak but, his face fell into his hands and he wept. Among the sobs, came muffled words from between his fingers, "God forgive me. God forgive me." After a few minutes, out came his handkerchief. He dried his eyes and cleaned his glasses. "I'm sorry to show myself up. I feel such a fool."

My wife knocked on the door and brought in some tea. He and I sat there drinking it, engaging in small talk and then he said, "I suppose you want to know what this is all
about."

"Only if you want me to know', I said.

"It was just after the war. I was married to a lovely girl. We were devoted. She became ill and was taken into hospital. She was so poorly, I could visit any time. I went every night after work and stayed until late. One night, I left the hospital a bit early. I had the washing to do. I'd not been home half an hour when a policeman knocked on the door. He told me that my wife had died just a few minutes after I'd left her. I let her down. I wasn't with her."

Harry's head fell back into his hands. For half a minute, neither of us spoke. I was praying silently with my eyes open. "Please take me seriously", he said. "Everyone says I did nothing wrong. They say I couldn't have known. They don't know what a lovely girl she was. She needed me and I wasn't there!'

Harry's guilt feelings had persisted more than half a lifetime. It was not for me to patronise him by judging whether his guilt was real. For years, he had been told that he was not guilty and yet his conscience still burned. We got up from our chairs and walked to church. We knelt at the communion rail. I told him that God wanted to give him lasting peace of mind. He began to talk to God, telling him the story. It took time and he kept apologising for his emotion. I told him that God had all the time in the world.

I do not believe that Harry sinned against his wife on that tragic night in 1946. Nonetheless, he had become estranged from God by his guilt feelings. Now he was being reconciled. I quoted a verse from the first letter of John 1.9., "If we acknowledge our sins, he is trustworthy and upright, so that he will forgive our sins and will cleanse us from all evil". I then pronounced the absolution adding, "You are free. The Lord has forgiven and healed you. Your guilt can never return." He lifted his head. His eyes were still wet but his face was that of a free man. He had begun a new relationship with the father, unafraid to approach him again.

The inner city is a slippery pit. The strong and the clever climb out. The broken, the emotionally lame, the mentally disturbed fall in. The number of those who live here by choice reduces each year. The old remain here out of allegiance to a community which has long since disappeared. The young stay until they have saved enough for them move somewhere "better'. Many of those who want to get out are crushed by irrational fear and guilt, frightened to set foot in a church. There are many Harrys in our city but most of them never find peace.

As I watch the dawn from Assékrem, seated on that enormous stone chair, I pray: "Lord, I sin every day and you offer me pardon every day but it's not every day that I see the people in my parish receive that pardon. Instead, they are bowed down, believing that they must carry the weight of guilt as a punishment. I want them to have the experience of Paul from Nigeria and Harry the rent collector, but instead they are like our cook, Elijah, so ashamed of causing hurt that they cannot face you.

"They say the words of confession but can't receive forgiveness. They don't love themselves enough to receive pardon, nor believe that you can ever love them. The flagellation of repeated confession compounds their guilt. It destroys and distorts them. Even after the absolution, they are forced to cry for mercy in the Kyries. In the Gloria, they ask the Lamb of God for more mercy. The Prayer of Humble Access likens them to a dog under a table rather than a child seated at it. Then, after their redemption has been declared in the prayer of consecration, they plead for more mercy in the Agnus Dei and in the words, *I am not worthy*.

"From the cradle they have been told that they are not worthy. When Alice was a baby, her father bought beer for himself instead of milk for her. How can she feel that she is precious in your sight, when she is worth less than a bottle of ale? And what about the woman who was a victim of incest in her childhood. Like Lady Macbeth, she feels that she can never be clean. How long must she grovel? The confession for her is not reconciliation but condemnation. She hears the absolution but believes that it is for the woman next to her.

Gordon, too, needs no reminding. He thinks he hears, "You are evil. Everyone in this church is better than you." He's been brought up by his mum and a succession of *uncles*, one of whom beat him regularly. The mother's next boyfriend disliked him so she had Gordon taken into care. When he was seventeen, he moved into a bedsit. He did things for which he cannot forgive himself. He will not believe that you accept him but thinks that he is under condemnation for ever.

"Lord, so many folk in our city are crushed by guilt and a sense of their own worthlessness. They are pushed around and reminded daily that they are of no value. They find it more pleasant waiting at the dentist than in the dole queue or Housing Office. They are reminded of their place in society by the flats they are forced to live in, by the squalor of communal landings, by their poverty, by their inability to get anyone in authority to take them

26

seriously. And, in addition, they carry the burden of their past.

"If I were not bound by an oath of canonical obedience, I would omit the confession and simply pronounce the absolution. They need no reminders that they are sinners, only that they are forgiven. Conventional sermons on sin reinforce guilt feelings.

"Yet, Lord, the last thing they need is to be patronised by having excuses made on their behalf. Raymond Fung once said that *sinners* in the Gospels are those against whom society has sinned. The sin of a society is projected onto a few who become outcasts. There is some truth in that. But, putting blame on the system, the structures and the parents, does not free them from a sense of guilt.

"Lord, at one time, I might have sent those like Harry away and told them that they were feeling guilt for the sin of others. But I now know, Lord, that they need to meet you at your cross because it is only there that sin is dealt with. It is only there that they can find peace. It is only there they can feel accepted. Whether it's their fault or someone else's, they carry the burden and it is only they who can bring it to you.

"Paul, the little boy who taught us Hausa, sat at table with us and later was able to receive forgiveness. Elijah, our cook, who would not so much as take a cup of water from us, has remained estranged. Lord, thank you for allowing me to eat at your table and find peace and forgiveness. It took years for Paul and Harry to know your grace.

They are among the few. They are rescued in ones, but I see them in their hundreds. I am far away from them but I offer you these, your people."

The sun is now warm on my face. I close the prayer book and Bible and begin to walk the few yards back to the hermitage, casting an eye along the majestic panorama. I thank God for this peaceful environment. But, in truth, it is difficult to be at peace even out here when those you have left behind are in torment. "Lord, it may take years for each of them to find your peace, but may just one more find forgiveness and peace of mind today."

3 Gloria

*Glory to God in the highest, and peace to his
people on earth.*

I first felt the compulsion to visit Assékrem
in 1974 when I was crossing the Sahara Desert on
foot. The walk began on Christmas Eve at Benni
Abbes, 1,000 miles north-east of Assékrem, where
Charles de Foucauld had built his first fraternity, and
where, at the time of writing, there is a community
of the Little Sisters of Jesus. By nightfall, on the first
day of that desert walk, I had travelled thirteen miles
south and was camped in the desert. In the early
hours of Christmas morning, I was looking out
between the tent flaps at the stars. The blackness of
the moonless night and clarity of the winter air made
the stars more brilliant and more numerous than I
had seen before. Without my spectacles, I saw them
out of focus - not pinpoints, but blurred discs, a
scattering of coins across the heavens. Their colour
and size varied while the atmosphere made them not
twinkle but breathe and pulsate.

For the shepherds on the first Christmas night, the
brilliant sky declared God's glory. For them, the
heavens and the sky were the same. When the angels
declared, "Glory to God in the highest heaven' (Luke
2:14), the shepherds would have looked at the stars.
It is the heavens, says the psalmist, that declare the

glory of God. And it was a star that marked the place where the baby was born.

Seeing the desert sky that Christmas, I thought of the angels who linked glory in the heavens with peace on earth. "Glory to God in the highest heaven and on earth peace". The angels both point down to the peace that the Christ-child brings and also direct our eyes to heaven.

The same earth-heaven connection is made in the Gloria. The angels' words are used at the opening to fill us with the wonder of God enthroned on high. They lift our eyes to heaven in a hymn of praise before declaring peace on earth. "Glory to God in the highest, and peace to his people on earth." The Gloria goes on to praise the Son as being one who brings peace to earth, though peace is not directly mentioned in connection with him. It is hidden in the words, "Lord Jesus Christ … you take away the sin of the world". What else can bring peace to earth better than the removal of sin? Eyes fixed heavenward ask for an end to sin on earth.

On that Christmas night in the desert, my thoughts turned from the shepherds to my family. I wanted to see my children unpack their stockings. I wanted to go to church with my wife and return home to Christmas lunch. I was homesick. If I could have waved a wand, I would have been plucked from the desert like a latter-day St Philip and dropped on Salford.

I looked out of my tent again and remembered my courting days. Joan was a student in Exmouth and I was in Durham. At prearranged times, we would each go to a telephone box and chat for a couple of shillings' worth of time. We missed each other and were always more sentimental than I can admit without embarrassment. She used a phone box on the promenade and sometimes described the view across the estuary with the moon reflected in the water. Whenever she did, I pushed open the telephone box door. This was misleading for the students queueing outside. They thought either that I'd finished, or I wanted more change, or that I wanted to know the time. No, I just wanted to look at the same moon that Joan was describing. Even though it wasn't reflected in water, it was the same moon. The fact that we could see the same thing at the same time made us feel close.

As I looked at the stars over the desert, I knew that they would be shining over Salford, cloud permitting. They brought me nearer home. The stars, like the rainbow, are an umbrella over all. As God's glory is manifest in the heavens over all, so is his desire for peace for all. The angels declared both in the same breath.

The stars encircling the globe remind me that the peace that the Christ-child brings is for all. We see his glory in the heavens and think of his peace on earth. As God sends the blessing of rain upon the just and the unjust, so he offers his peace to all. The stars shine over labour camps and holiday camps. They are over those who have drunk their fill and they are over those who are dying of thirst. They are over those who sit on a restaurant terrace, eating foie gras and they are over those who hunger. The prisoner away from home in a distant land looks out and sees the same stars as his or her mother. Whoever we are, wherever we are, the heavens are over us declaring God's glory and reminding us of his desire for peace.

That first desert crossing is now sixteen years behind me. I have returned to Algeria, stayed at Assékrem and am on my way home, stopping for a holiday in France. I am at a table on the terrace of a restaurant in the Dordogne, a region famous for its cuisine. There is too much artificial light to see many stars but I can just make out the Eagle constellation in the south. I take a sip of wine - a 1985 chateau-bottled Cahors. Its excellence takes me by surprise and I savour it. "There's the Serpent, just above the horizon!" I say. My eyes are getting used to the light. "This salade Dommoise is out of this world. I love goose gizzard and walnut oil. And, that's the Waterman!" I am half out of my seat peering forward. "If Alain looks out from Assékrem, he'll see it much higher in the sky there."

I think of Tuareg boys, guarding their flocks, looking up at God's glory in the heavens like David the shepherd boy. "You reckon that looking at God's glory in the heavens makes absent friends feel closer?" asks a voice within me. "It can assure them of God's desire for peace on earth?"

"That's what I said."

"So, if I'm in a foreign gaol, I can look through the bars and say, 'God bless my old mum. There's the pole star. If she goes out to bring in her washing, and looks north, she'll see the pole star 52 degrees above the horizon, like a message from God, bringing us closer together?'"

"You've got the point."

"And you were getting all sentimental about Tuareg shepherd boys looking up at the Waterman. It reminded you of David the shepherd boy writing Psalm 19: 'The heavens declare the glory of God'. What about the Tuareg shepherd boys who have watched their herds die because of drought? Do you suppose they're looking up at the Waterman, saying, 'I bet there's someone, somewhere eating more than he needs, looking at the stars and getting sentimental over them while we starve'?"

I stop looking at the sky, lest my Perigordian delicacies should become unappetising. I begin a conversation on the music of Edith Piaf, a subject suited to eating *Confit de Canard*.

4 Ministry of the Word

This is the word of the Lord.

I read the collect and sit down. Somewhere in the pews is a lesson reader. I don't know who it is; I haven't checked. Nobody steps forward. I look appealingly at the congregation. A Voice comes from the back. "It's Alice's turn, but she's gone to her daughter's." Ah, but there's Fred getting to his feet. He strolls to the lectern, takes his glasses from his pocket, fumbles to find the page and reads from an epistle of Paul. He reads quickly and in a monotone, pausing only at difficult words. It comes out so gabbled that I can't take it in. Then he says, "This is the word of the Lord" and I wonder how the Lord can be so unintelligible.

During the last verse of the gradual hymn, the acolytes escort me with their candles to the lectern. I read the Gospel and then preach. The sermon is ill-prepared.

The Eucharist is ministry of word and sacrament. We meet God in both. It takes faith to believe that we meet him in bread and wine while it can take a suspension of the critical faculties to believe that he comes in gabbled readings and in the ramblings of preachers.

It is now January 1975, and I have walked 300 miles south from Benni Abbès where the Little Sisters of Jesus have their fraternity. In this part of Algeria there is no blade of grass, let alone a tree. There are no hills, neither houses nor hermitages and not a rock bigger than my fist - worlds apart from Assékrem. It is still the Sahara Desert only there isn't any sand. I am alone fifty miles south of Reggane walking across one hundred miles of reg - desert which is as flat as a lake, hard under foot and covered with a sprinkling of shale, like the football pitch I played on as a child. It is so flat and empty that I don't seem to be getting anywhere. The horizon ahead never gets any nearer. The one behind is never any further away. I have to tell myself that I am making progress, though I feel like a mouse on a treadmill.

The emptiness is both unnerving and liberating. I am so used to landscapes with features that my mind superimposes things that aren't there. I remember the red shale football pitch from my childhood. I now see football pitches going into infinity in every direction, with their goalposts white against the ochre dirt. That image disappears and I superimpose onto the desert a picture of the ocean. I am in a rowing boat rising and falling with every wave. The featurelessness of the landscape removes mental inhibitions and stimulates the imagination. It seems legitimate to imagine the absurd.

There are no fences on the land, nor any around my behaviour. There are no police or psychiatrists to inhibit me, no friends or public to criticise. I can do or be what I want. I am liberated. I sing weird songs of spontaneous composition. I talk to myself and then I preach to a congregation of my imagination, saying whatever meaningless sounds come into my head. Sense does not matter. My mind is getting rid of its waste. What comes out of my mouth is not from my consciousness. Nor is this speaking in tongues. I claim no divine cause for it and yet, as the sounds come, I know that they express something. I don't mean that they are in code or in a foreign language, nor that they are capable of being interpreted. They are an expression of my psyche. If my friends were here, they might say, "Geoff's had a breakdown".

This desert sermon makes no sense and there are no hearers but it is doing me some good. It is cathartic, the mind offloading itself. Having delivered hundreds of sermons and having listened to hundreds more, I wonder whether my preaching here in the desert is any different from my preaching in church. Preachers respond to an urge to open their mouths, while much of the time congregations daydream. We preachers console ourselves. It says in the Scriptures that God's word shall not return void. And St Paul exhorts us to preach in season and out of season. It is not for us to worry if anyone hears. I must obey the command. Woe unto me if I preach not the Gospel. In this way, the preacher justifies his or her own need.

I am in Shambles Square in Manchester, a small square with pedestrian access only. One can cross it in thirty seconds. It is bounded by a pub and shops and has good acoustics - a favourite spot for buskers. Today there are no buskers, only a preacher. Hollywood could not have produced a better stereotype. His black, floppy Bible is resting open on his left hand, while his right hand beats the air.

I hear no more than thirty seconds of the sermon but the rapid succession of clichés shows that its subject is 'salvation'. I go into a shop, buy a birthday present for a friend and come out. The sermon is still in progress. It is well structured, using logical building bricks - if you grasp the first point, the second one follows and the second point leads to the third. Yet, the preacher doesn't seem to mind that nobody stops long enough to follow the thread. I watch him from behind. He and I are the only stationary people in the square. People are walking through hurriedly, avoiding his gaze. Nonetheless, he is preaching as if he has an audience. Words and hand movements are directed at a non-existent watching crowd. I am reminded of my preaching in the Sahara Desert and wonder what are the forces that compel words to spew forth when no one listens?

Good Friday afternoon, 1985. Two dozen Christians - Anglican, Roman Catholic, Pentecostal and Methodist - are carrying a wooden cross through Salford. At pre-planned points, we stop and deliver a homily. We arrive at Salford's new shopping precinct. Shoppers are out in their thousands. We have chosen this spot so that we will be seen and listened to.

The sermon is for non-Christians, but not one passer-by stops. Though the shopping precinct is crowded, there is a cordon sanitaire of ten yards around us. People side-step the preaching of the word and make a beeline for the ice cream cart and fish and chip shop. The longer the preacher drones on, the more tempted I am by the smell of the fish and chips. I feel like sneaking away and joining the queue. It's not just that I'm hungry. I feel awkward and out of place. I wish God would pick up the preacher and drop him in the Sahara Desert. It wouldn't be so embarrassing for him there. I remember the preacher in Shambles Square and wonder if anyone's looking at us like I looked at him. What are those forces that compel words to spew forth when no one is listening? Better to pack up and go.

I am presiding at the Sunday Eucharist. It is the second Sunday after Easter. Verses from Revelation are read telling us of the joy of those who are invited to the wedding supper. The Gospel reading is from Luke 24, the road to Emmaus. I preach on Jesus becoming known in the breaking of the bread. We do not see Jesus through natural eyes: we can only see him when the Spirit reveals him to us. As I preach, I wonder what the Spirit is revealing to the congregation. At least they laughed at the joke, but is Jesus being made known? Their faces don't give away anything. At the end of the service, I ask two teenagers if they can remember the theme of my sermon. They can't. I turn to a man in his thirties and ask him the same question. He answers by retelling the joke. I ask an older woman the same question. She, too, begins by mentioning the joke. I remember the man in Shambles Square. Week in week out, I preach. What are those forces that compel words to spew forth when so few listen? Guilt? Fear? A desire to please God? Exhibitionism? Egoism? At least in the Sahara Desert there was no pretence.

One Advent Sunday, I am the guest preacher at a nearby church. I have prepared the sermon well and am pleased with the delivery. Later in the service, the incumbent gives out the notices and then says, "I now invite our guest preacher to give his testimony'. I squirm, resenting the invitation. I have neither agreed nor been warned. I am not too keen on the giving of testimonies, but more than that I think, "How dare he spring this on me? Wasn't my sermon enough? If we believe that God inspires the preacher, then why add to what has been preached? I've preached my heart out!"

I know the tradition of this church. He wants an outline of my Christian pilgrimage. Grudgingly, I get on my feet. I feel that I have nothing to say. The words are spoken with resentment.

In 1988 I take my congregation by bus from Salford to Israel. We are not allowed to drive anywhere without an official guide. Ours is a Jewish Israeli called Judy. One day, as we pass a settlement, she says, "That is Emmaus, where the risen Jesus made himself known to two of his disciples". She does not preface what she says with, "According to Christian tradition," or "The New Testament records". It is simply, "That is Emmaus, where the risen Jesus made himself known. " There is a murmuring on the bus. "She's a Christian . . . she's a believer." Everywhere, she uses the same approach, "This is the street down which Jesus carried his cross" and "This is the spot from where he ascended and to which he will return". Her words are like a sermon, building up the faith of the hearers. One day, when our party has gone to buy cold drinks, she is leaning against the bus smoking a cigarette. "Judy", I say. "You talk as if you believe what you tell us." She hesitates and then speaks with a smile that is almost a smirk, "We are well trained. Besides, when you earn $80 a day, it doesn't pay to upset the clients. When I take Jewish groups round, I'm a Jew. When I take Arabs round, I'm a Muslim."

"Do you practise your own faith?"

"No, I'm an agnostic." Some of our group never found out. They received her words gladly.

I am invited back to the church where I preached and grudgingly gave my testimony. After the service, a young woman comes to me with her husband and says, "I want to thank you for what you said last time you were here. I wasn't a church-goer and I'd had my arm twisted to come. Your words knocked me for six. I became a Christian and so did my husband."

"I remember that sermon well', I said.

"It wasn't your sermon! It was your testimony!'

The word of God has a dynamic of its own. God chooses to speak in spite of the intentions of the preacher.

I am invited to concelebrate at a patronal festival. A call from the hospital prevents me from arriving in time to take part, but I arrive late and sit at the back. I uncharitably judge the sermon to be a mixture of waffle, platitude and oratory. The words are a smoke screen, obscuring rather than revealing God.

Later in the worship, I see a smoke screen of a different kind, as incense smoke surrounds the sacrament. The cloud tells us that there is something here greater than bread and wine. The incense is overdone and though I can hardly see the altar, I believe that the sacrament is there somewhere among the haze, conveying to us something of Christ. Is it then too much to believe that among the smoke screen of the preacher's words there is something of God?

The word of God is to the sermon, as Christ is to the Christian. Some Christians are dotty and well-meaning. Others are intolerant, rude and arrogant. And yet, almost to our surprise, we find Christ in them.

The word of God has a dynamic of its own. God chooses to speak in spite of the intentions of the preacher. The Spirit blows where he will.

5 Intercession

Merciful father, accept these prayers for the sake of your Son, our Saviour Jesus Christ.

At the Eucharist, we are guests at the King's table. In the intercessions, we ask him to extend his rule beyond that table into our lives, families, neighbourhood and across the world. Feasting at the King's banquet, without interceding for those who are absent, is as obscene as eating dinner without concern for the starving. And interceding to God to help those whom we can help is an abrogation of our discipleship.

6 The Prayer of Humble Access

We do not presume to come to this your table,
merciful Lord, trusting in our own righteousness,
but in your manifold and great mercies. We are
not worthy so much as to gather up the crumbs
under your table. But you are the same Lord
whose nature is always to have mercy. Grant us
therefore, gracious Lord, so to eat the flesh of
your dear son Jesus Christ and to drink his blood,
that we may evermore dwell in him and he in us.

The linking of manifold and great mercies to a homely metaphor - a dog waiting for scraps under a table - makes the *Prayer of Humble Access* the favourite of many. As we begin to say it, members of my congregation who have been daydreaming wake up. Though they are moved by the prayer, they give little thought to those gathering crumbs outside -- the alcoholics drinking cider against the church wall.

Late on a Saturday night, I am preparing a sermon, getting to grips with a difficult yet well-known Bible story. I read between the lines to find a reason for Jesus' apparent hardheartedness. He sets out for the pagan territory of Tyre where he is not so well known. He wants to be alone with the twelve. They are having difficulty grasping the message. A year or two of his teaching and they still misunderstand. They are blind; he has no interest in political power, nor in overthrowing the Romans. He does not want a war horse or servants or a palace. He believes in a kingdom where the weak are as important as the strong and where women and children are as important as men. The twelve should have got the message long ago. He has demonstrated it by touching the unclean and treating foreigners like humans.

Jesus has found a quiet place in Tyre. Maybe he can now get the twelve to understand. They are sitting attentively on the floor when a woman bursts in. What woman dares interrupt? She prostrates herself pleading for Jesus to heal her daughter. Jesus could never turn away a woman whose child is suffering, but the twelve have a different idea. Women do not burst in on a gathering of men. She should have sent her husband. Her place is in the kitchen or with her children. Even worse, she is pagan. The twelve are not finding the teaching easy, but they resent interruptions. They think that they have exclusive access to Jesus.

The Syrophoenician woman wails while the disdainful twelve look on. Jesus knows their thoughts - "Get rid of her! We are learning about the kingdom! The sons of Abraham will lead the world! Pagans will be slaves! This heathen woman can no more share in the kingdom than can a dog in the king's banquet!" They want her turfed out.

Jesus could admonish the twelve, as when he said, "Let the little children come to me" (Mark 10:I4).

This time he wants the woman to speak for herself, so he voices their thoughts. "Can I take what belongs to my children and feed it to a dog?"

The woman shows no resentment at being called an unclean animal. She knows where she stands with these foreigners. "Even decent folk don't let a bitch starve", she says. "They give it scraps."

I have a dog. He's called Alf, has three legs and sleeps in the kitchen. On a winter's night, I go to bed content that he is not in the cold.

After fourteen years at one Salford church, it is time for me to move on. One month before going to Assékrem, I accept my bishop's offer and move from my inner-city parish to a neighbouring one. The new church, thanks to the laity and my predecessors, is beautifully maintained, an oasis in the middle of an Urban Priority Area. It's a picture-postcard of a church. Around it, what was an untidy graveyard is now a well-kept lawn. It is a 'Waterloo' church built of Yorkshire stone in 1832 and has a fine tower and belfry. It stands on high ground which once looked out over farm land, but now looks out over tower blocks and maisonettes, the sanitary slums of the 1970s.

The railings or lack of them around the churchyard is the only imperfection. Over 160 years, they have rusted and fallen or been taken down. Even that will be remedied. The city council is to replace them, not with rods of mild steel, like those around playgrounds but with a replica of the ornate 1832 originals.

The interior of the church is bright and the decor impeccable. The heat is on twenty-four hours a day, seven days a week, so it's warm and comfortable.

Round the exterior of the building are ventilation grids for the cellar. Through one of them comes a blast of warm air from the boiler. If there were ten degrees of frost, you could stand naked on it and stay warm. It has been discovered by homeless alcoholics. In cold weather two or three of them sit over it with their bottles. At night they sleep there. There is no public toilet nearby and so they foul the churchyard under cover of night.

They are sprawled there in their stinking and stained clothes as we come to church. Dishevelled, drunk and dirty, they are surrounded by chip papers, bottles and cans. They spoil a near-perfect scene and, though they have never been violent, they terrify the old and the very young by their appearance. Within days of my induction, a handful of folk ask me to get rid of them.

I have a dog. He's called Alf, has three legs and sleeps in the kitchen. On a winter's night, I go to bed content that he is not out in the cold.

After only twenty-nine days in my new parish, I set off to Assékrem to keep a longstanding engagement. I leave behind the question of alcoholics in the churchyard, but know that I will have to take a stand one way or the other when I return after three months.

In the heat of the day, I sit in the hermitage by a small window. An open Bible and prayer book are on the table in front of me. I am struggling with the Prayer of Humble Access. "Lord, we're not fit to gather crumbs from under your table, but we still feast in your house. Can the unworthy inside deny crumbs to the unworthy outside? Can we who have been dragged from the hedges and alleys, show no mercy to those we have left behind?"

The crumbs of our Eucharist are not bread and wine, but heat from the flue. If someone doesn't use that heat, it will be lost. If we deny alcoholics heat, we will be like those who put scraps in the bin while the hungry dog looks on. If the police evicted them from the churchyard, we would be masking the problem, sending it down the road, not alleviating it. While the alcoholics are with us, they are a reminder of our inability to address sickness in society. They show up our failure to be salt, light and yeast. If they were to leave us, we could remain insulated from the sin, pain and sickness in the world and we could get

back to congratulating ourselves on the beauty of our
building and its worship.

"And yet, Lord, leaving them and their filth in that
draught of warm air is not doing them much good,
either. What sort of life am I encouraging them to
lead? I am a sentimentalist. That warm air is a
substitute for the gospel that I am at a loss to
interpret for them. If I cleared them off, they might
be forced to find hostel accommodation. But, I have
a nagging doubt that they might end up in someone
else's doorway."

I pick up a pen, make a few notes and step outside.
I look down the boulder-strewn mountain side to the
valley below. In it is the dry bed of a stream beyond
which a dusty volcano rises with a basalt plug
growing from it like a molar from the gum. Behind
that, half lost in the haze, dozens of eroded, titanic
forms are thrust up from the earth. I scan the
mountains, valleys and rocks. Nothing moves. I am
far away from people and their pain in everything but
thought.

The three months spent at the hermitage and
on holiday is now up. In preparation for my return,
the congregation has cleared the churchyard of
bottles, cans and excrement. As I am walking to
church for the first time after my return, I see, from
the distance, that the city council has put up the
railings. They are ornate, with stout spirals topped
with cast-iron flower heads, painted black and

bronze. They are sturdy and pleasing to the eye. On three sides of the churchyard, there are double gates to match. As I enter those on the west side, I stop and grasp them. They seem to be made to be touched. I examine the newly forged metal and then hold them at arm's length looking them up and down. The railings and gates cost £110,000. As I admire them, I wonder how many homeless alcoholics could have been given shelter for the cost of them. I tell myself that they would not be homeless if they had not spent their money on drink. Then I wonder if it is fair that their sin robs them of their homes and families, but my sin does not rob me of mine. And, to what extent is an addiction a sin, anyway?

I grip the metal bars. Did Mary waste the ointment she poured on Jesus? Is it wrong to adorn at great cost the place where God is worshipped? Is not worship the act of showing God his worth? Isn't he worth £110,000? I look at the railings admiringly. They put the finishing touches to a fine building. I loose my grip, walk down the church drive, and am greeted by folk chatting outside the west doors. "I can see you like the railings", says one of them. "You'll be pleased to know that while you've been away, the church council has decided to padlock the gates when the church is not in use."

I have a mental picture of a winter night. A dishevelled man, bottle in hand, has his face to the padlocked gates, watching hot air rise.

I have a dog…

7 The Peace

*Christ is our peace. He has reconciled us to God
in one body by the cross. We meet in his name and
share his peace.*

The evening sun is warm on my back as I
pick my way over boulders on my way down the
escarpment. I'm climbing down from the hermitage
into the valley to take a closer look at one of the
extinct volcanoes. The only noise is that of my
breathing and the sound of rubber soles on rock. The
troubles of my congregation are far away. Without
other people, everything is beautiful. Here, at
Assékrem, I am at peace with an absent world.
Then, my foot finds a loose rock. Before I know it, I
feel the impact in the middle of my back as I fall. I
pick myself up, ranting at myself for my stupidity.
There is no one else to blame. I have brought discord
even to this place, thus destroying the delusion that,
were it not for others, there would be peace on
earth.

It is a Saturday afternoon in my church hall.
The hall has been built within the church building,
using what was the rear of the nave. The east end of
the building is untouched and is our worship area.
Worship and social functions take place in different
parts of the same building. Our youth organisations

are in the hall today setting up stalls for their Christmas fair. Fifteen or twenty people are arranging the stalls with bric-a-brac, soft toys, hand-sewn novelties, peg bags and the like. It is not a jumble sale, nor has it been advertised as such, but there is one rack of 'good-as-new' clothes, put there by our boys' club. Dora, our girls' club leader, sees it and is incensed, believing that second-hand clothes lower the tone of the fair. "Who put that there?" she asks without expecting or waiting for a reply. "This is not a jumble sale! I'm not having a load of old rags spoiling the display." With that, she grabs the rack and wheels it briskly out of sight through the double doors that lead into the nave aisle.

Brenda, who had put the rack there was in the store room. "Funny", she thought when she returned. "I'm sure I put the clothes rack out." She hunts around, finds it in the nave aisle and puts it back in the hall. Dora walks over to her, furious.

"I'm not having it! I'm just not having it! This is a Christmas fair, not a rag sale."

"Do you mind?" pipes up one of the helpers, "some of those clothes were mine. I paid good money for them. They're good as new."

Dora goes on as if she has not heard, snatches the rack and drags it out of the hall and back out of sight into the worship area. No one dares challenge her. "It's just not good enough! I'm not having it!"

It's ten to two and the sale starts at two o'clock. I've had my lunch and am walking the three hundred yards from my house to the church building. All the doors are locked and a crowd is waiting at the west doors. I let myself in with my key at the east end and am walking up the nave aisle towards the doors that lead into the church hall. I see the rack of clothes and, assuming that they have been forgotten, wheel them out of the worship area, through the doors, into the hall. Dora rushes at me and grabs the other end of the rack. I keep tight hold, sensing her aggression, but not knowing why. "It's just not good enough', she begins and then tells the tale. I tell her that while she might not like clothes at her sale, it would have been better, to have reached an agreement in advance. Furthermore, I am tired of clothes being stored in church. I want them offered for sale so that the remainder can be disposed of. She does not listen. "I'm not having it! This isn't a jumble sale!' I am about to lose the tug of war with the rack, but am rescued by the man on the door. He lifts the barrier and the crowd floods in. Both women dash to defend their stalls, leaving me with the rack.

That evening, when we have cleared up after the fair, I go to see Mike, a member of my congregation. Over the years, I have spent many hours with him. I have seen him come to faith, baptised and confirmed. We spend much time in each other's homes and, on Sundays, after evening service, we go jogging together. He is a likeable man, but has a quick temper. He is thirty years old and powerfully built. Before he started coming to church, he spent his free time engaging in Thai boxing. Even now, he spends hours each week working out in a gymnasium.

Tonight, I go to his house with a feeling of foreboding. I have given information to the police which has resulted in his being charged with a violent offence against another parishioner. Mike cannot understand how I could do this to him. For my part, I am an eye witness. I haven't told the police anything heard in confession nor in a counselling session. I told them what I saw.

There is a risk in going to see him, but there are issues which must be discussed. As we chat on the doorstep of his small terraced house, the tension mounts. He is becoming more and more angry. Then he hits me in the face, smashing my glasses, and causing a swelling. I walk home in a daze. I have given evidence against my brother in Christ and he has retaliated. I remember David who would neither lift his hand against Saul, the Lord's anointed, nor against Absalom, his own wayward son. Has not Mike been anointed by God? Is he not his child? I have driven a wedge between us that prevents me from helping him. My feeling of sorrow alternates with that of anger. One moment I forgive him; the next, I feel violent.

9.20 next morning, I walk into church for the ten o'clock Eucharist. Ernie, one of our regulars, is already there, polishing the nave floor with an electric buffer. "Ernie', I say, "I appreciate what you're doing but, please, not on a Sunday morning." Ernie wheels the buffer away and I go into the side chapel to pray in preparation for the Eucharist. The blow to my head has left me with a headache. As I pray, my emotions still alternate between anger and sorrow. At ten to ten, I leave the side chapel. The prayer time has made me feel worse, focusing my mind on the problem rather than on God.

Nine minutes before the Eucharist, I walk towards the vestry, ill-prepared for worship. My mind should be on higher things, but I remember that I need to find out how much we made at yesterday's fair so I can announce the total. I see Brenda and beckon her to find out from her. Before I speak she says, "That woman! I'm not having her talk to me like that! She's so rude! Who does she think she is? After you'd gone, she had another go at me." I try to console her, but soak up some of her feelings.

I am walking towards the vestry when Ernie comes to me. "Do you know what Dora said to me? She said that I had no right to be polishing the floor on a Sunday morning. I stopped when you told me to, but thought that I'd give the kitchen a quick going-over. There was no harm doing the kitchen. When I refused to stop, she took the plug out. I have as much right to do what I like in this church as she has." I tell Ernie that he was a bit naughty and should not have provoked Dora. I look at my watch. Five to ten I must put on my vestments. I am almost at the Vestry when one of our guitarists stops me, "Can you tell the organist not to choose hymns out of the chorus books without consulting me. Ancient and Modern's best for the organ. I'm doing the communion hymns and there's a clash." I listen, agree to speak to the organist, and take two paces towards the vestry, but come face to face with a fuming Dora.

"Will you have a word with Ernest? He was buffing the floor this morning. When I told him to stop, he was most rude!"

Half an hour later, I am on the chancel steps saying, "Christ is our peace. He has reconciled us to God in one body by the cross. We meet in his name and share his peace. The peace of the Lord be always with you."

"And also with you," replies the congregation.

"Let us offer one another a sign of peace." There is spontaneous movement as the congregation shares the peace. I should walk down among them, but feel unable. "Lord, I am nauseated by this hypocrisy. I've just said that you've reconciled us in one body by the cross. It's just not true! We are not reconciled. I'm involved in a feud with Mike. And look at Ada, every week, she avoids Marie. She's so subtle, always clasping the hand of someone else when Marie goes by. Mind you, Marie is relieved. There's never been any love lost between them.

"And look at that! The audacity! Those two who've just kissed each other are sworn enemies! If it were true reconciliation, I'd weep for joy, but I know that their aversion to each other hasn't stopped. And what about me? I try to love them all, but their pettiness exasperates me. If they were all thieves and dope smokers, I could more easily forgive them, but their bitching makes me bitchy, too. Even worse, I'm still seething at Mike. I'm not being honest if I share the peace."

"Geoff, they are not as bad as you think. And even if they were, it wouldn't matter. When that unmarried sixteen year-old became pregnant, there was no bitching, no judging. They rallied round. What about when Vera was ill? Her lifelong feud with Anne ended with a hospital visit and a few flowers. And what about Damien? Everyone knows that he has a criminal record and yet he is welcomed like the rest. Let me tell you about a Eucharist at which I was president.

"There was a congregation of twelve. They had been my students for almost three years and were now at the end of their training. They were not like you when you were an undergraduate - ten hours of lectures a week and half the year on vacation. They had been with me most of the time, preparing to teach and to lead. It shouldn't have been difficult for them to learn but they were slow. They should have got the message easily. After all, I had lived for them. I wanted them to forget about themselves and to live for me and for each other.

"I understand your exasperation, Geoff. I did everything to get my followers to see. Teaching wasn't enough! Nor were miracles! They couldn't shake off their old ways. When I was tired of their squabbling, I picked up a child and placed it in the circle and told them that if they wanted a part in my kingdom they had to be like him. They said they understood, but they didn't.

"I went to Jerusalem to take the message of the kingdom to its logical conclusion. I was about to die and still they wouldn't stop squabbling. On the night of our final meal, we were tired and grimy. Tension was mounting in the city; we were all feeling it. When we arrived at the place where we were to eat, they were too proud to get water and a towel. Instead, they argued about who should sit next to me.

"After the meal, I consecrated bread and wine. Within a few hours, all but one would disown me, but I wanted them to eat and drink of me all the same. I gave communion even to the one who betrayed me. As he received it, I let him know that I knew what was in his heart. When I gave him the bread, I was giving myself to him. He was taking me to do with me what he pleased. I gave myself unconditionally. That is what I do in the Eucharist.

"Later, I was in the garden. The quietness was shattered by the thunder of cavalry and foot soldiers, a thousand in all. He led them to me and exchanged with me the kiss of peace. The peace I gave him was unconditional. It was not dependent on his accepting or returning it. Now, Geoff, do you think that you can go down the chancel steps and do the same?"

8 Bread of Life

Blessed are you, Lord, God of all creation.
Through your goodness we have this bread to
offer, which earth has given and human hands
have made. It will become for us the bread of life.

The Little Brothers of Jesus at Assékrem usually live in community in the cluster of stone shacks near the original one built by Charles de Foucauld on the southern face. Only Alain is there at the moment. Edouard has returned to France for an eye operation and Michel is visiting Tuareg camps. My borrowed hermitage is a mile and a half away from theirs on the eastern face of the mountain. Those hermitages which, like mine, are used for retreats, are out of sight, and a good way from each other. Their locations have been well chosen. They are below the rim of the plateau, on the edge of the escarpment in the few places where the descent is steep, but not sheer. From them, one may easily walk the few yards to the top or scramble with difficulty down into the valleys. Being just below the rim of the plateau, they are out of sight of the rest and protected from the worst of the wind.

In the evenings, I go for a walk westward across the plateau without seeing anyone. When I have clattered for half an hour over the hot stones, I arrive at the escarpment on the other side, similar to the one I've just left. I look out from it across more rocky valleys, extinct volcanoes and basalt plugs. In every direction is rock and dust. My hermitage is built of stones, not one of which is hewn. Shelves, ledges, cubby-holes, bed, steps and walls are all of a piece, knitted together with stone into the mountain side. The living quarters and chapel are separate other than being on opposite sides of a common wall. Their roofs - corrugated iron, covered with flat stones - channel the four inches of annual rain-fall into drums from which the rain is syphoned into smaller containers.

The chapel has the same dimensions as the living quarters, seven feet by eleven feet. On entering, the only chair, two slabs of rock covered by the pelt of a brown and white goat, is to the left, against the back wall. In front of it is a kneeler - goat skin draped over a board. The altar is a two-feet wide rock on top of another making the shape of a mushroom. On it, there is a red candle, bonded by its own wax to a 'candlestick' - a rough stone. In eight places, slabs protrude from the wall to make ledges. On one of them, behind the altar, there is an icon of the face of Christ. On another there is an 8 inch high African Madonna in plaster of Paris, once white now ochre with the dust of the desert. There is a tattered habit hanging at the back, also once white now ochre. Near it, is a hole in the wall where the vessels are kept covered by a square of embroidered fabric. Behind the altar are two windows, each a foot square, one of which has a cross in stained glass mounted against it.

I sit on the chair of rock and goat skin. The adrenalin which has driven me two and a half thousand miles drains away. For a moment, my eyes rest on the icon, then on the Madonna and then on the candle, but always they return to the stones that are this place - the altar, walls and shelves. The habit, candle, icon and Madonna are points of contrast that show me that I am in a world of stone.

I stand up, light the candle and go behind the altar. I have never celebrated the Eucharist alone before. I am not sure I believe in doing so. My head is full of questions about the status of that which I am doing. What is this bread that now rests on the palm of my hand? Is this Eucharist valid? In what sense is this Christ's body? How and in what form is he present? There are no answers, but as I look at the bread, the questions disappear. The bread is on my hand, waiting to be eaten, but I cannot bring myself to eat it immediately. I am content to look at it. I have not eaten for almost three days. I wanted to fast in this place of stones so that I may learn what bread is.

I am on a mountain of stone, in a hermitage of stone, before an altar of stone. Outside, the mountain top is covered with stones, like round flat loaves mocking the hungry. Here in my hand, this tiny piece of bread confounds the barrenness of this place. In my hand there is that which gives strength to the weak, that which feeds the world. Though it is small, it speaks louder than mountains of bread and rivers of wine. Yet it is the stones of this place that make this bread speak. A small kindness done in a caring community goes unnoticed, but in a concentration camp it is a symbol of all kindnesses. So, this small bread is all bread for all time, for all people.

It is the dryness of this place that gives the wine its power to refresh. It is the insignificance of a Galilean peasant that makes him God. It is his weakness that gives him power. So, too, it is with this insignificant morsel.

I hold the bread in my hand and see there the God who created, sustains and saves the world. I see food for the hungry, strength for the weak, power for the powerless. I am not bothered whether bread has become body or whether it remains plain bread. Let the theologians argue. Those issues are as sterile as the stones of this place. All I know is that I look at bread, but see God.

9 Sanctus

Holy, holy, holy Lord, God of power and might, heaven and earth are full of your glory. Hosanna in the highest. Blessed is he who comes in the name of the Lord. Hosanna in the highest.

I step down into the chapel and lower myself almost to the floor, into the chair of rock and goat skin. The candle is unlit on the altar. I use it sparingly. There is none to replace it. My eyes no longer dance around, looking at every nook and cranny. They are used to the place. Rather, they rest on a stone here or an object there. They light upon the icon behind the altar. The face portrayed is that of the man from Nazareth. I am much more at home with him than with our ascended, glorified Lord.

"Jesus, friend of sinners, you are ascended and glorified. We read in Revelation that you appeared to John. You were wearing a white robe and a golden belt. Your head and your hair were white, your face like the sun, and your eyes, burning flames. Your voice was a terrifying roar with a sword shooting from your mouth.

"If you could come to me as Jesus of Nazareth, I'd introduce you to my friends in the market and pub, but if you came as recorded in Revelation, we'd run in fright. It was even too much for the apostle John. He had leaned against you at the inaugural Eucharist and had later seen you die but, when he saw you glorified, he fainted.

"Jesus, I understand the nature of your holiness when you were incarnate. You were holy, set apart to do your father's will. Sometimes, that meant being profane in the eyes of religious people. You touched the unclean. In those days, I could have sat down with you and felt at home. I could have brought to you William, the homeless alcoholic and Deborah, the single parent. They would have felt accepted and loved.

"But now that you are ascended, glorified. It's as if you are the God of Isaiah's and Ezekiel's visions rolled into one. Your voice terrifies like the shout of an army. Your presence is fiercer than a raging fire. You are unapproachable. Your holiness is not just a set-apartness to do the will of the father. It is a brightness at which I cannot look. The Sanctus fills me with awe."

"Geoff, the sun is 93 million miles away. If you get much nearer to it, you will be incinerated, but that doesn't stop you from enjoying the sunshine. My ascended glory is a bit like that. It is awesome. And yet, you catch no more than an inkling of it in the Sanctus. Surely, you can sing of my glory from afar and appreciate me as you appreciate the sun on a spring day? That's not too dazzling. I do not want to frighten you with my presence. Why do you think I choose to meet you in bread and wine?

"When it comes to meeting me in glory, that's a different matter. The apostle John fainted when he saw me. Yet, will I not revive you as I revived him? Will I not do the same for the alcoholic and the single mother? I bent down and touched John; he knew the hands that had blessed the children and healed the sick. And you will know them, too. You will know my voice as I say to you what I said to him, 'Do not be afraid. It is I'."

10 Real Presence

The Lord is here. His Spirit is with us.

Charles de Foucauld used to spend five hours a day in prayer, much of that time adoring the blessed sacrament. He met Jesus in bread and wine. Here at Assékrem, I have found an empathy with his spirituality. Back home, the presence of Jesus in the Eucharist has been much more elusive.

"Lord, if you are present in the Eucharist, please tell me where I may find you."

"Do you not know that I am everywhere? I am with you on Assékrem, in Salford and as you journey. If you go to the bottom of the ocean, I am there. If you fly to the most distant galaxy, I am there, too. I am in every moment of the Eucharist, every place and every movement."

"Lord, to be everywhere is to be nowhere. Folk would find it strange if they saw me looking for you under the altar frontal. I know that you are everywhere but where is your presence focused?"

"In the Eucharist, you can find me in many places. I am, for example, in the midst of my people. You know the Scriptures, *'Where two or three are gathered in my name, there I am in the midst.'*

"Lord, I don't want to be obtuse, but the middle of the congregation is halfway up the centre aisle. When I look there, all I see is parquet floor."

"I am in my people. I live in the hearts of all believers."

"But when I look at Alf, for example, I see only an old man with arthritis."

"Then look for me in my word."

"That's hard when Fred is reading the epistle. The words come so fast that I can't take them in. At best, I learn about you. But, even then, it's Fred or St Paul telling me about you. I don't want to hear about you. I want you first hand. I want your voice, not theirs."

"Do you not find me in the sacrament?"

"In bread and wine I see only symbols of your presence."

"What about when the bread is broken and the wine poured? And, do you not see me when it is shared? I became known to Cleopas in the breaking of bread."

"I know about Cleopas, but it doesn't work for me. I cannot find you anywhere. I am like a pantomime character. The audience shouts to me, "He's at the window." I turn round and you duck out of sight. Then they shout, "He's in the doorway." I turn round and you've stepped behind the set. I am not so fortunate as those who can point to where they see you in the Eucharist. "Lord, you gave me eyes but I don't see you!"

"I didn't give eyes to you so that you could see me! I gave them so that you don't fall down the altar step with the chalice! If you look for me with your eyes, you will never see me. Don't be disappointed if l don't appear. I will be there. You might not see me, but you will see evidence of me."

So, I come to the Eucharist, wondering what evidence of Jesus I will find. As I administer the bread, the first person at the communion rail is Amy, eighty years old. Next to her is three-year-old Carmen, waiting to receive a blessing. Her sticky fingers clutch a lollipop, while she swings on the rail. Brian, a thirty-year-old school teacher, is next to her. Then comes Harry. He can neither read nor write and lives in a squalid bedsitter. Debbie, a local journalist is next and then William, the homeless alcoholic, followed by Susan, a single mum. Shoulder to shoulder with her is Paul an electronic engineer, followed by Ron, who has recently been convicted of theft.

Where Jesus is present and how he is present in this Eucharist, is still a mystery to me. But, that he is present is beyond doubt. Only Jesus of Nazareth could gather together round one table such beautiful and diverse people. The Lord is here and his presence is with us.

11 One Body

Though we are many, we are one body,
because we all share in one bread.

With no radio, no newspapers and few books to occupy me, my mind is in reflective mode most of the time here at Assékrem. Reflection often turns to reverie. I am sitting on the throne of rock, built outside the hermitage. My eyes focus on the gigantic barren monoliths, but I am miles away. Day in, day out, a fragmented church declares itself to be whole.

As I walk to church on Sunday mornings, two retired men lift their hats as they are on their way to Mass at the Church of The Mother of God. Not far behind them is Mr Wyatt on his way to a neighbouring Anglican parish. Christians locally and across the world are on their way to worship. Millionaires in Beverley Hills will soon be waking to drive to church. Villagers in rural Africa and India are walking over the mountains and through swamps heading back home after worship. As I am walking to my church, I am over-come by gooey sentiment as I contemplate the worldwide church at worship. We may not be together in one building, but we who are many are one body because we all share the one bread. At least, that's the theory.

A missionary steps out in faith. Before he has any converts, he builds a school in a valley where the territories of three tribes meet. On the day of enrolment, not one child turns up. Not disheartened, he goes to the tribal heads and asks them why they are boycotting the school. They say that they do not want their children corrupted by the practices of neighbouring tribes. The missionary then invites the tribal heads to meet on neutral territory to resolve the problem.

They sit under the stars round a fire. The missionary says, "Let us try to understand each other. Let each of you say why you do not wish your children to attend the school. Will you explain what is so special about your way of life that it cannot be influenced by the other tribes?"

The first man stands. "My people have nothing against the other tribes so long as they stay in their own territory. As for our traditions, they are derived from the highest divine authority. They must not be corrupted.

"We are the people of the forest. When a boy child is born, we catch a wild boar and offer it as a sacrifice to the great Baobab tree in the middle of the forest. In token of the fact that all the animals of the forest belong to that tree, we take the tusks of the boar, climb high up the tree and drive one of them like a nail into the trunk. This bonds the child to the forest. The mother keeps the other tusk until the day the boy becomes a man. It is then sharpened and used to cut a scar in each of his cheeks. These scars represent the tusks of the boar. The man then wears the tusk on a cord round his neck.

"The forest will not allow a man to enter it if he does not bear the scars and wear the tusk. We, the people of the forest, have a duty to drive out intruders and keep our traditions pure. We have many other customs: when we go hunting, we always say that we are not going hunting in case the spirits of the animals are listening; we may not eat fruit under a full moon; we may not take a spouse from outside our tribe. These and all our traditions are sacred. They were given to our forbears by the highest authority. If we wanted to change them, we could not."

The first man sits down on his log and the second one stands. "My people have nothing against the other tribes so long as they stay in their own territory. As for our traditions, they are derived from the highest divine authority. They must not be corrupted.

"We are the people of the savannah. When a woman is in labour, she is chased by the women out of the village into the bush. If she is strong and the baby is healthy, she will return with her child. All children of the savannah are born in the savannah. They belong to the savannah and the savannah belongs to them.

"Small boys go hunting with the men, but when a boy believes that he has reached manhood, he declares it before the village. He is given a spear and sent into the savannah. He may not return until he has killed a large, dangerous animal. When he has done so, he lights a fire with much smoke. The men of the village see the smoke and go to him to carry back the animal. While the men are away, the women select a bride for him. He is married on his return. There is feasting and dancing. His cheeks are scarred in lines like the scratch of a lion, to show that he has fought a dangerous animal.

"Some youths never return from their expedition. Some stray from the savannah into the forest and are killed by the forest people. We have many other traditions: we may not give our children eggs to eat; if a cow becomes sick, it must be driven into the savannah and not allowed to return; we may not take a spouse from outside our tribe; strangers who do not have the scratch of the lion are not allowed to hunt in the savannah. If they are seen, they are hunted down. These and all our traditions are sacred. They were given to our forebears by the highest authority. If we wanted to change them, we could not. We have a duty to keep our traditions pure and to drive out intruders."

He sits back down on his log and the third man stands. "My people have nothing against the other tribes so long as they stay in their own territory. As for our traditions, they are derived from the highest divine authority. We cannot change them.

"We are the people of the river. The river is the mother of the anga fish and the anga fish is the mother of the river. They give us life and death. When a baby is born, it is taken from the mother and thrown in the river while she looks on. Before she can rescue it, she must pause to eat a roe of the anga fish. The roe of the anga is the life of the river. It takes only a moment to eat it, but until the mother has done so she may not wade in the water to rescue her child. If the child survives, she knows that the great river has given it life.

"We have many other traditions: we may not fish for one month before the great rains; we may not use a net to fish; we may not take a spouse from outside our tribe. These and all our traditions are sacred. They were given to our forebears by the highest authority. If we wanted to change them, we could not. We have a duty to keep our traditions pure and to protect the river from alien tribes."

"For goodness sake!' screams the missionary. "All this is a bit primitive! Tribalism's on its way out. You've been a republic for thirty years. You're all members of the same nation. Even more, have you never read the Scriptures?" He opens the Bible and reads: *'There was a huge number, impossible for anyone to count, of people from every nation, race, tribe and language; they were standing in front of the throne.'* Don't you see? This is God's plan for the world! All the tribes will be gathered before God as one. With God, there is only one tribe. And listen to this from the Book of Galatians (3:28), *There can be neither Jew nor Greek, there can be neither slave nor freeman, there can be neither male nor female — for you are all one in Christ Jesus!* If it were written today, it would read, *There are neither Forest People, Savannah People nor River People. All are one in Christ Jesus."* '

The three shake their heads and say in almost one voice, "All our traditions are sacred. They were given to our forebears by the highest authority. If we wanted to change them, we could not."

The missionary goes back to the little church where he is the sole worshipper. He gets on his knees, prays, gets up and goes again to see the tribal heads. For months he exhorts them. He pleads, he cajoles, he preaches from the Scriptures. At last, he sees the penny drop. The tribal heads are converted and baptised. Many of the ancient traditions are abandoned, children from the tribes go to the mission school and begin to intermarry. On Sundays, the three tribes gather to share the Eucharist. With one voice they say, "Though we are many, we are one body, because we all share in one bread."

The missionary goes home on furlough, loads up his hatchback with slides, projector, screen and tape recorder. Every congregation he visits is moved by his story. Superstition and tribalism have been defeated by the power of the cross. He travels the country, but is especially well received by the churches of his home town who pledge to double their missionary giving to support his work.

Then, just after his return to the mission field, a meeting is convened in his home town by the bishop. The bishop believes that the town is too small to have three churches of the same denomination. He has already asked the churches to work out a way of amalgamating, but all three have refused. He now summons them and asks them to explain themselves.

The bishop opens the meeting by reading a prayer and then says, "Let us try to understand each other. I now invite a representative from each church to say what is special about their tradition and what it is that prevents amalgamation." The first person stands.

"My people have nothing against the others so long as they continue to worship in their own building. As for our tradition, it is derived from the highest divine authority, namely that of Scripture. We may not alter it one jot or tittle. It is our duty to keep our tradition pure and to protect it from corruption.

"Our beliefs must remain untainted. We will join with the other churches only if they will undergo initiation. Initiation is through conversion. They may join us only through new birth. After new birth, our people will then listen to their account of that event for signs of authenticity. They must say how they have entered into the light by receiving forgiveness through the shedding of Christ's blood. The mention of receiving a new peace and joy is more important than having those qualities.

"If the others join us, we must regularly hear them using catch phrases such as, *Praise the Lord* or *Praise his name*. It is more important to say these words than to live a life in praise to God. Converts must learn their passwords well. They must never meet a fellow member without using one of them. There are hundreds of passwords, but here are a few*: prayer meeting, evangelism, salvation, preach the word, the gospel, bless, brother and sister*. These words are like secret hand-shakes. Used regularly, they ensure continual acceptance. And, though it is important for us to have a daily time of devotion, it is even more important for us to signal to other members that it has taken place."

The first sits and a second stands. "My congregation has nothing against the others so long as they worship in their own building. Alternatively, they may join us if they accept our tradition. It is derived from the highest divine authority, namely that of the teachings of the church. Woe unto us if we alter it.

"We will amalgamate with the others if they will become as we are. They are free to join us. There is no initiation. If they have been confirmed, they may declare an allegiance to us. To join, they must regularly attend Mass at a church known for the purity of its ritual. We believe that all Eucharists are equal but some are more pleasing to God than others. Attendance at, and love of, those acts of worship that separate us from Protestantism are essential. We are enraptured by processions of the blessed sacrament, benediction, concelebrations, crownings of Our Lady and incense, especially if it's overdone.

"We gain instant recognition by other members by mentioning Walsingham, lace cottas, and fiddle-back chasubles. We always address priests as "father". Even priests, address each other as "father" when they wish to signal membership.

"Divisions in the church are acceptable and necessary other than the rift between Canterbury and Rome. Whenever the ordination of women to the priesthood is mentioned, hysteria is permitted.

"Members may smoke and drink beer. We may take a spouse from any tradition, though it is more acceptable for women to marry than men. If a male member declares that he is to be married, an appropriate response might be, "Good Lord! What for?" In most other matters, we exert no influence over each other's private lives except that we are suspect if we refuse to go to the pub when other members invite us."

The second speaker sits down and a third stands. "My congregation has nothing against the others so long as they are allowed to worship in their own building. Alternatively, they may join us if they accept our tradition. It is derived from the highest divine authority, namely that of the Holy Spirit. Woe unto us if we alter it. Tradition and rigidity must not put a straitjacket round the Holy Spirit.

"You may join us, if you speak in tongues, though we will admit you if you say that you hope to receive this spiritual gift soon. After you have joined us, you must greet other members with a hug, inane grin and heavenward roll of the eyes. You will not be allowed to be negative about anything other than worldliness. If a sister says that her husband has been promoted, we say, 'Praise the Lord!' If her husband dies, we say, 'Praise the Lord! Your husband has been promoted to glory!'"

"In our worship, we prefer disposable choruses – learn them today and throw them away tomorrow. We like to sing about victory. We do not have church choirs. We have music groups. Any instrument is allowed, though the organ is the least preferred. We love flutes and violins, but a guitar and tambourine are mandatory. The liturgy of the Eucharist is acceptable. Otherwise, all worship is off-the-cuff - er spirit-led.

"When praying to the first person of the Trinity it is important to address him as *Father God*. If you use *Heavenly Father*, God *our Father*, or simply *Father*, you may be mistaken for an evangelical. Failure to comply with one of the least of these rules will make one suspect, and people will condescend to pray for one." With that the speaker sits down.

At the end of the meeting, the bishop feels that the churches are even further away from each other than they were at the beginning. He returns to his palace, disheartened. He enters his private chapel, gets on his knees, prays, and goes back to see the church leaders. For months he exhorts them. He pleads, he cajoles and does everything, but preach from the Scriptures. He sends round the rural dean, the archdeacon and members of the diocesan pastoral committee. After some months, he announces his retirement.

The leaders of the three churches rejoice. They have resisted the works of the devil and the machinations of the bishop. On Sundays, they join with angels and archangels, but not with the folk down the road. Each congregation says, "We are one body', believing that the 'we' refers only to themselves. Totems continue to be revered and taboos avoided. Life is comfortable again.

12 Credo

We believe in one God.

I have happy memories of attending church as a teenager. Billy Platt, a fellow chorister had been bought a new-fangled transistor radio for Christmas. He put it in his pocket and listened to it all through the church services by means of an earplug. The wire ran under his cassock, coming from under his collar to the earpiece. So long as the ear plug was jacked into the radio, no sound came out of the speaker. On one memorable night, as the creed began, his posture straightened, putting tension on the wire. The jack was pulled out of the radio, treating a bemused congregation to a choirboy doing a hurried strip, in search of the radio, while Frankie Lane sang *Ghost Riders in The Sky*. That was the first time in my life that the creed had come to life. I was in adulthood before it gained an importance of its own.

I am at the end of my time of solitude at Assékrem. I've spent time praying, reading and writing, each evening I've gone for a walk across the plateau or along the northern edge of the escarpment. Today, as usual, I am up before dawn, but this time I pack my rucksack with my few belongings. I check the stone shelves of the hermitage in case I have forgotten anything, open the heavy, wooden door for the last time and step outside. The edge of the escarpment is twenty yards up the slope. I scramble to it and then pause to take a last look back at the shack that has been my home. It is only a few yards away, but camouflaged against the rock of the mountain side.

Then, I turn and walk south-west across the plateau, listening to the rocks clatter under my feet. The mountain reminds me of Kinder Scout in the Peak District, a featureless table top, except that instead of peat bog, there is baked clay covered in a crazy paving of loose rock.

It takes me twenty-five minutes to get to the cluster of stone shacks inhabited by the Little Brothers of Jesus. Alain, the tall French Roman Catholic priest, is still the only brother in residence. Before I began my time of solitude, I spent a little time chatting to him over a cup of coffee. He has been here fourteen years. I didn't realize that hermits could be such good company. I listened with fascination as he told me about the Tuareg, camels and meteorology – at the time of writing, he runs the weather station at Assékrem which Charles de Foucauld founded in 1911.

His hermitage is perched on the south-facing rim of the plateau, looking out at more sterile mountains and eroded volcanoes. Next to it is the original one built by Charles de Foucauld, housing a chapel. As I reach it, I am about to end my time of solitude. It is a quarter of an hour after dawn and mass is scheduled to begin.

I lower my rucksack to the ground, kick off my shoes and step inside, out of the chill dawn air. It takes my eyes a moment to get used to the dimmer light. The chapel is no more than fifteen feet long and there is no furniture The floor is covered with rugs and goat skins, like that of a Tuareg tent. The walls are dry-stone. They radiate a gentle heat, absorbed from yesterday's sunshine. The altar is a thin slab, supported by three pillars - each with the cross-section of an irregular hexagon. Not one stone of the walls or altar has been hewn.

Alain is sitting on the floor near the altar. He stands, clasps my hands and greets me with a silent smile. He is wearing an alb – or is it a Tuareg robe? His stole is broad straw-coloured, of a heavy weave and without pattern or motif. His feet are bare.

He sits back on the floor, cross-legged, on a goat skin. I, too, sit on the floor, facing him, two yards away. He says the liturgy slowly, almost in a whisper. It is as if he is leading a meditation. His speech is relaxing, hypnotic.

He is Roman Catholic and I am Anglican. Canterbury and Rome are not in communion. The division seems even more absurd here than at home. The nearest town to here, Tamanrasset, has a population of 80,000 with not one indigenous Christian. There are two French sisters and a priest there. Another priest is travelling with the Tuareg.

When there are so few Christians among so many
Muslims, denominational divisions seem especially
strange. Yet, 'the church militant here in earth'
keeps our communions apart. In my time in Algeria,
I have enjoyed Arab and Tuareg hospitality.
Wherever I have been, strangers have offered food
and shelter, but they have always been the host and I
the guest. Alain and I are not host and guest, but
family.

The way Alain officiates takes my mind off the
division. Then, he asks me to read the Gospel. He is
prevented by canon from offering me the sacrament,
but he offers me what he can. So, we share the
word. As I read the Gospel, whose proclamation is
common to both of us, we are bound together by it.
Then, in the creed, we say that we believe it. Not
one word divides us.

I want unity expressed in bread and wine, but I find
a greater unity here than in shared sacraments, a
unity which has primacy over other forms, a unity
which must exist before bread and wine can be
shared. It is the unity of those who own Jesus as
Lord. Before the body of Christ can receive its
expression in the sacraments, it must first be
authenticated by a common gospel. Such is
expressed in the historic creeds of the church. And
so, Alain and I are one in Christ. We share a perfect
expression of that oneness as we say, "We believe."

Cults and sects have Eucharists of a kind. As I say
the creed today, I know that this Eucharist is
endorsed by the one, holy, catholic and apostolic

church, founded by Christ and of which Alain and I are both part. It is only if I can share the creed, that I can hope to share the sacraments. It is the affirmation of the creed that makes us brothers in a way that I am not a brother with the Tuareg or with my agnostic neighbour. Yet, we who are one are prevented from sharing the sacrament. To my surprise, I feel no resentment today. I have found a unity which the canons of the church can never take away.

I am still sitting on the goat skin two or three yards from the altar. Alain is standing at it, taking bread and wine. I thought that I would feel excluded, but I do not. The unity we have found in a common gospel makes me content to watch, knowing that one day our shared assent to the creeds will bring our two traditions together around the Lord's table.

Alain puts down the chalice, closes his eyes and puts his hands together in prayer. I wonder what he is praying. He opens his eyes, takes the paten on which some bread remains and looks at me. We are looking at each other, wondering what the other is thinking. He is standing with the paten in his hands. I remain on the goat skin, knowing that, if I go forward, he will not refuse me the bread. I must not allow myself to compromise him and so I remain on the floor.

We are still looking at each other, wondering. Then, he beckons. I am not sure if I have understood the gesture. He beckons again. There is no mistake.

He is asking me to come. I get up awkwardly and step forward.

13 Our Father

As our Saviour taught us, so we pray.

I say to my children, "If you do something shameful, never be frightened of owning up to me. I may disapprove, but I will never turn my back on you. Whatever you've done, no matter how much it hurts me, I will never reject you."

If I, a sinner, who sometimes neglects his children, can show them mercy, how much more merciful is our God in heaven. If I stole church funds, committed an indecent act, ran off with a choir girl, smoked dope, was sent to gaol, engaged in transvestism or took a bottle of communion wine and joined the alcoholics in my churchyard, the bishop might defrock me, my family might disown me, my congregation might reject me, my colleagues might ostracise me, my friends might keep clear. But there is one to whom I could turn. Jesus destroyed the idea of a tyrant in heaven. We may approach our creator with confidence. We are bold to say "Our father."

14 Bread into Stones, Wine into Water

We pray that this bread also may be to us his body.

I am attending a Eucharist in a fifteenth-century church. The time, date and place are unimportant. The church is packed. Bread, rather than wafers is being used to emphasise the connection with the Last Supper. On the altar, are thirty cottage loaves, ten flagons of wine and many chalices. One loaf and two chalices would be enough, but each communicant is given bread the size of a tennis ball and ample wine to wash it down.

The bread takes two or three minutes to eat. I am so occupied by the mechanics of eating and drinking that the spiritual content is lost. Jesus is far from my thoughts. I do not sense the body and blood of our Lord. I am drinking spiritual water, eating spiritual stones. The miracle of Cana has been reversed.

It is midnight communion, 1962, at my boyhood church in Manchester. The red brick building stands among terraced houses which run uninterrupted for miles. After the prayer of consecration, Derek Gisburn is the first out of his pew. We have never seen him in church before, but there are no surprise appearances at communion on Christmas Eve. All the teenagers in the choir know Derek. He stands out from the local labourers and warehouse workers - he wears the only toupée in the neighbourhood and it has remained ginger longer than his greying back and sides.

He has never been confirmed, though the rector does not know it. Derek hears the words, "Drink ye all of this". Though he is first at the rail, he wipes his mouth on his sleeve and hands the empty chalice back to the bewildered celebrant.

The Victorian church is full. Attendances are normally high in Denton, a hatting town outside Manchester where I am serving my second curacy, but today there is a three-line whip - the archdeacon is the preacher. The rector is ill and I am celebrating.

Two large chalices are consecrated. I administer the bread, the archdeacon, the wine. It is our custom to let all but the frail take the chalice in both hands. The archdeacon has a different practice. He keeps hold of it. Barely has it touched the lips of the communicants and it is whipped away. Some do not receive at all, having intended to wait until the archdeacon has let go before taking a sip. I avoid the eyes of those who make a silent appeal in my direction.

The communion hymn finishes and I give the last few folk the bread. I return to the altar to find a full chalice untouched. To consume the elements at the end of a Eucharist, may be the decent, tidy and correct thing to do when finishing a few remains. On this occasion, it seems like debauchery.

I decide to leave the elements on the altar, proceed with the service, and during the final hymn take the chalices a few paces down to the choir and ask them to assist me. The archdeacon places the second chalice, one quarter full, on the altar. I look up at the congregation, clear my throat and am on the point of saying, "Let us pray" when he whispers to me, "Consume the elements!"

He might be an archdeacon, but I am the celebrant. He has no authority in the context of this Eucharist to tell me what to do, but I don't reflect on that. He has a deep cultured voice and his tone, if subdued, is that of a military command. I, the curate, act on reflex and obey. Before the silent gaze of two hundred people, I drink the lot.

It is a November evening. Deborah and Susan, two of our choir girls, are sitting in my lounge for their final confirmation lesson. In previous weeks, we have learnt a little of the doctrine and practice of the Christian faith. Now for the mechanics of receiving communion. I demonstrate the traditional ways of receiving bread and wine. We practise with a plate and cup. For some of our teenagers, the Eucharist seems to be little more than engaging in an adult practice forbidden to children - drinking wine. "Remember", I say, "You only take a sip. When you receive communion, you are taking Jesus into your life. You don't receive any more of him by taking a big gulp."

As they go through the front door, I remind them to turn up early for the confirmation service. "Be here at a quarter to seven, on Friday! Don't be late!" They walk down my path on the way home and when they think I can't hear they say, "It's not fair! You only get a sip!" I sigh. Has my teaching failed? Is the Eucharist for them no more than under-age drinking?

Lord, you are devalued when the symbols of your presence are made commonplace. We seem able to change wine into water and bread into stones.

I am seated on a goat skin two or three yards from the stone altar. Alain is standing at it, making his communion. I thought that I would feel excluded at this moment but I do not. He puts down the chalice, closes his eyes and puts his hands together in prayer. I wonder what he is praying. He opens his eyes, takes the paten on which some bread remains and looks at me. We are looking at each other, wondering what the other is thinking. He is standing with the paten in his hands. I am on the goat skin on the floor, knowing that if I go forward, he will not refuse me the remaining bread. I must not allow myself to compromise him and so I remain where I am.

Then, he beckons. I am not sure if I have understood the gesture. He beckons again. There is no mistake. He is asking me to come. I get up awkwardly and step forward. As I receive, I see that there is no wine in the chalice. It contains water. But, for me, this is the miracle of Cana.

15 Sharing as Receiving

Receive the body of Our Lord Jesus Christ which he gave for you.

It is blisteringly hot. The sun is bouncing back from the sandy ground like heat from a fire. One hundred and ten in the shade, but there is no shade. It is 1975 and I am in the scrubland of Niger on the southern edge of the Sahara. I have walked 1,600 miles south from Benni Abbes where the Little Sisters of Jesus have their fraternity. A month ago, I passed within twenty miles of Assékrem, pausing only for a moment to look up a mountain pass in its direction.

Kano, my destination, is now a fortnight away. I trudge on, anxious to make good time over difficult ground. There is sand underfoot and thorn bushes all around. At a quarter to ten in the morning, while I am eating bread and pork paté, a Fulani bush man leads a donkey towards me on which his wife and baby are riding. He lives the way his ancestors have lived for generations. He wears clothes made of skin and a hat of straw. We greet each other in the language of the Hausa people and I oblige him with water, pouring some into his gourd. He is travelling in my direction, so off we walk together.

After a few minutes, he stops and unravels a bundle of dirty rags. It smells of sour milk. Inside is a muddy paste in a Calabash bowl. "Millet?" I ask.

"Yes. You take it?" he says, scooping some with his fingers and offering it to me. It looks like clay ready to be thrown onto a wheel. Should I eat it? I am in two minds - we being many are one body because we all share the one bread. In what sense am I one with this man? I look at the awful brown sludge on his fingers and ponder.

I am administering the chalice. The congregation is singing a communion hymn. The sound is thin. Some are chatting, others queuing in the chancel, and others are at the rail. There are sixty or more people in church, fifteen of them children, some old folk, three graduates, and two or three adults who can neither read nor write. One or two of the congregation rarely take a bath; some are fastidiously clean; some refuse the wine when they have a cold; others bring their germs to the cup.

Ernie, from the old folks' home, is the last person at the rail. He can hardly walk and has a brain disease. Usually, when he drinks, he dribbles. I could give him the sacrament by intinction, dipping the bread in the wine, but he is my brother in Christ, not my half-brother in Christ. I give him the chalice. He dribbles. Moments later, I consume the elements, contaminated wine and all. We are family and share one cup.

I have been driving along the M6 motorway for four hours. I pull into a service area for a cup of tea and a sandwich. The only table that is vacant is cluttered with the remains of a meal. There are a few chips and baked beans on one plate. I would prefer chips and beans to the sandwich I have bought, but I do not eat food left by strangers. If the food had been left by one of my children, I would not have hesitated. Nor do I hesitate to share plate and cup with my sisters and brothers in the Eucharist.

The Holy Communion reminds me of my status, or lack of it before God and my fellows. It is a symbol of Christ on the cross. God, I believe, beckons humanity to kneel before that cross in shame and adoration. In shame, because Jesus, the only good man, is murdered by a world which we all help to make cruel. In adoration, because the love and forgiveness he shows, as he hangs there, heals us of our guilt and divisions. None is so good or great that his or her place is not before the cross. It is only when I, the worthless, bring my vanity and emptiness to that cross that I find my true worth, the worth of knowing that God loves me.

The cross is the great leveller. Everyone needs the healing and forgiveness which the crucified Christ brings. Before him, prime ministers, brain-damaged children, Fulani bush people, homeless alcoholics, mass murderers and saints can find first their emptiness and then their fulfilment.

The bread is the body of Christ, broken, the wine his blood, poured. As I kneel to receive the sacrament, I am kneeling, with countless others, before him. I can bring only worthlessness and can lift my head higher than no other. Yet it is only here, forgiven and healed, that I can lift my head at all. The shared, unwashed cup is a symbol of Christ's love, given not only for me, but equally for all.

The Fulani is holding out to me his meagre food. He is not a Christian, nevertheless he is a man for whom Christ went to the cross. The fact that he does not recognise it, does not mean that God loves him less. He and I are not Christian brothers, but we are loved by the same father. He might not want to receive the sacrament with me but this calabash of millet has become bread and wine. Sharing this food is a sacrament, a recognition not only that God has accepted the Fulani, but also that he has accepted me. How can I receive God's love, if I will not acknowledge that God loves this man, too. If God accepts and loves him, then so must I, and I must eat the millet.

Every day in my ministry, I am asked to give signs that I accept the people whom God loves: Tea in a dirty cup; An embrace from a smelly person; The threat of personal violence or the loss of my wallet.

The Holy Eucharist is not an act in a vacuum. It brings together all that we are outside formal worship and it sends us out from our worship to express what we have experienced in our worship. How can we share the Eucharist if we are not prepared to share our lives outside our worship? How dare we drink from the same cup if we are not willing to drink the cup of common experience? Sharing the cup on a Sunday morning is a blasphemy if I cannot share the cup of experience with people God loves.

It is Sunday and I am sitting at the kitchen table writing about the Eucharist. Harry, a member of our church, walks in with three carrier bags of food which he scavenged yesterday from the dustbins at Salford market. One bag is full of squashed cream cakes. He declares that he found them uncontaminated in a single bin liner. The last time he gave that assurance, I found cigarette ends among them. He goes to the kitchen cupboard, takes out two plates, puts the cakes on them and offers me some. My children make sounds of disgust.

Harry and I have a slice each, avoiding a piece that looks gritty, washing it down with coffee. The hand-written draft of this meditation is in front of me. "Here, listen to this, Harry. It's a comment on the cream cakes", I say, and read him my account of the Fulani and his millet and the passage about the Holy Communion. We laugh.

The Fulani is still holding the mud-like

millet on his fingertips, offering it to me. We are standing looking at each other, motionless and silent. How can I refuse? I shake my head. I have failed my idealism, because of my will to survive. I am doubtful of the water with which the millet is mixed. The cost of the common cup has proved too high for me. We who are many are one body if we dare to share the one bread.

16 Sharing as Giving

May we who share Christ's body, live his risen
life; we who drink his cup bring life to others; we
whom the Spirit lights, give light to the world.
Keep us firm in the hope you have set before us,
so we and all your children shall be free, and the
whole earth live to praise your name.

I am still in the scrubland of Niger, alone
and on foot, pressing on towards Kano. The sun is
high in the sky and sweat is trickling down my neck.
I sit on a rock to begin my lunch of dry bread and
water. A herd of about two hundred sheep appear
from among the thorn trees and come plodding
towards me, churning up the sandy ground. They
are driven by three men in long nightshirts. These
men are not wearing shoes - they can't afford to wear
them out on a long trek. They only put them on in
town.

The men are gaunt, underfed. They come to me
and exchange a long African greeting, their hungry
eyes never leaving my bread. Five minutes, and they
are still with me talking to me about the problems of
herding sheep. Their eyes never leave my bread.
The Lord says, "Is not this the sort of fast that pleases
me... Is it not sharing your food with the hungry?"
(Isaiah 58:6-7)

It is teatime Sunday 11 February 1990. I've been working on a report all afternoon, that is when I've not been interrupted by the telephone and callers. William the 62 year-old alcoholic has re-emerged. He resigned himself to sleeping rough during the summer, but since the autumn he has been round here often. He is sitting in the porch eating a chicken sandwich and drinking a cup of tea. He has been here four times today. I have made a number of fruitless telephone calls on his behalf. We are back to square one. He cannot find a place to stay tonight. Last night, he slept on the landing of a block of flats. In the last year, he has lived in almost a dozen places and has been thrown out of all of them. Even the Salvation Army won't have him. Sometimes, he is evicted for fighting, but usually he is thrown out for non-payment of rent. He drinks and smokes the benefit money given to him by the government. Three days after he gets his money, he is spent up and so borrows from friends. When he draws his money half of it goes immediately on repaying what he has borrowed. After a few weeks, he is so far behind that he has not enough to pay the rent. Before long, he is back on the street. Then, I or someone else find a little cash, pull a few strings and find somewhere for him. A few weeks later, he is out on the street again. Time and again, I have found him a place to stay. Time and again, he has been evicted. Each time, it's harder to find him somewhere. Now it's almost six o'clock on a winter evening and he is in my porch with nowhere to go.

For the past few weeks, he has been worshipping with us, receiving the sacrament. I am in a quandary. Is he a brother or a vagrant? We keep open house. Folk from the parish walk in and out at will, but vagrants are kept at the door. It hasn't always been like that but hospitality has been abused so often. We have had things stolen from us by people to whom we have been in the process of giving. Food was stolen by a man we were feeding in our kitchen. My shoes were stolen by a man to whom I had given shoes. Those he stole would not even fit him. But it was when our children's Christmas money was stolen that we resolved to keep vagrants at the door. It was a popular decision. Our children have always been unnerved by the presence of unwashed people of dubious odour. William has never stolen from us and is now a worshipper. Some of the folk at church have no idea of his background. He is just another member of the congregation to them. The problem for us is that he doesn't smell too sweet and is incontinent when he's drunk.

Upstairs, we have a guest room. It's warm, nicely furnished and has a wash basin. If other members of my congregation were on the street, I would offer them the room. But why should I do what his own family won't do? His son lives round the corner and won't have him in his house. He says that his predicament is his own fault. So does the Salvation Army and those who run various other hostels.

The skier is not told by the hospital that it will not treat him because the broken leg is his own fault. "You shouldn't have gone skiing! We'll keep the bed for more deserving cases." The man with the heart attack is not turned away from the hospital because he has eaten butter and not sunflower margarine. We are not refused God's mercy because we are sinners. When I hold out my hands for the sacrament, I come as a sinner, no less than William. If I got all I deserved, I'd roast in hell.

I go to evensong, return and William still in my porch. I make more phone calls on his behalf. By ten o'clock, I have run out of leads. William has not budged from my unheated porch. Upstairs our guest room is warm and unoccupied. I go and put the kettle on.

The eyes of the shepherds are still on my bread. The Lord says, "Is this not the fast that I want, that you share your bread with the hungry?"

"Lord, I have some more bread. Can't they have that?"

"But that's a week old! It's mouldy!"

"Lord, if I share my fresh bread, we'll all end up hungry. Isn't it better for at least one of us to be full than all of us to be part empty?"

"But why should you be the one who is full? Give your fresh loaf to one of them that he may be full."

"But it's my bread, Lord, and they are used to being hungry." It is now my turn to look hard at my

threatened loaf, not daring to sink my teeth into it lest I make my
selfishness too obvious.

"Is not this the sort of fast that pleases me? Is it not sharing your food with the hungry?"

An afternoon in December 1989. It is cold, not much above freezing. It has been windy and raining all day. When it is almost dark, the phone rings and a young woman speaks to me in tears from a coin box. "It's Deborah Turner." I prepared her for confirmation. She was in the choir. She is unmarried, twenty-two, and has a year-old child. "Can I come and see you?"

A few minutes later, I open the front door. She and baby Catherine are soaked. She has been walking with the pushchair for hours in the winter rain. The pushchair has no cover. The baby is crying, her pale skin red with cold. Deborah's brown hair is drenched, matted and stuck to her face. Her clothes are heavy with water. They come in. The Vicarage is warm and bright with Christmas decorations. They sit in front of the gas fire, their outer garments steaming on the fireguard. Deborah bursts into tears. "My boyfriend left me a few days ago and my sister owes me ten pounds. She should have paid me yesterday when her giro came, but she'd spent up on Christmas shopping before I could get to her. I've no milk for Catherine and no food in the house and no heat. I've no money to put in the meters. Catherine wouldn't stop crying. She was hungry and had dirtied her nappy. I've no money for food and no clean nappies. The flat was cold. The only way I could stop her crying was to go for a walk. I've been walking for hours."

I leave the room and alert my wife. She brings a fresh disposable nappy, mixes baby milk and puts it in a bottle. Deborah changes and cleans up the baby while I bring her two pounds to buy more nappies. I give her two pounds more to put in her meter. "If I give her too much", I think, "she'll waste it." I deliberate, "Should I give her more? If I give her much more, I will be as poor as she is. It's easy to share a cup on Sunday mornings, but how can I share all my money? Lord, I am being ripped apart. I want to cling to my security and I want to cling to you." I think of Jesus who gave all he had, so that we who are poor might become rich.

I try to ignore my conscience by making myself busy. She needs food. I can do a little to help though we don't keep many tins. "How many days before your giro arrives?" I ask.

"Three', she says. I get a carrier bag and open the kitchen cupboards.

"Though we are many, we are one body because we all share in one bread." I look in the cupboard at two tins of tomatoes, three tins of beans, a tin of ham and a tin of tuna. Next to them is a tin of salmon for Christmas.

"I'll give her a tin of beans."

"What about the salmon?" the Lord asks.

"She might not like it and then that really would be a waste."

"You could ask her."

"But if she says that she likes it, then I'll have no choice but to give it to her."

"We being many are one body if we dare to share the one bread."

"But Lord, the salmon is special. It's for Christmas."

"What is Christmas if it's not for me? Aren't I special? Aren't I more special than anything else in your life? In as much as you have done it unto the least of these."

"I know that verse, Lord, but there are thousands like Deborah outside those doors. One or two of them come every day. If I allowed myself to see you in them, they could have the salmon, the tuna and the ham, the rest of the tins as well. Lord, if I could see you in them, I'd take down my Christmas decorations and give them to them for their drab homes. I'd empty my wardrobe. I'd sell my car."

"Well, why don't you, then?"

"How can I lie? I don't want to lose my comfort and security. You remember, Lord, the brass Christmas decoration like a miniature fairground carousel, the one with all those moving parts with little people holding hammers that played a tune on bells when it was placed on the mantelpiece above the fire. Those little brass people glinted in the fairy lights as they were driven round by convected air, playing music like the angels. You remember - it was my wife's and children's favourite decoration. We gave it away gladly to a family with no decorations. It brightened their dowdy home. They loved it, but sold it two days later. And what about my treasured leather jacket that I gave away to the man who had no coat. He wore it for work and it was ruined with cement within a day. He threw it in the bin at the end of the week."

I am still holding the empty carrier bag and looking at the tin of salmon. Dare I?

17 Dismissal

Go in Peace to love and serve the Lord.

The sheep are still foraging among the thorn bushes, the heat still radiating like fires from the sandy ground. The three scrawny men in their nightshirts still gazing at my fresh loaf. "Lord, I need that bread."

"So do they", he says. "They need it even more than you." I unwrap the week-old mouldy loaf, break it in three pieces and share it among them. They eat gladly while I sink my teeth into the fresh soft bread.

"See Lord, I told you. They don't know any different. They're happy for me to eat the good bread and they the bad. That is the order of things."

"I came', he says, "to change the order of things."

William is still in the porch. I go upstairs, get a mattress, an old sleeping bag and some blankets. I carry them downstairs, out of the front door and into our garage. As I move my children's bicycles to make some floor-space, my breath comes out in plumes in the ice-cold air. I put the sleeping bag and blanket on the floor. William beds himself down while I make him a cup of coffee. When I bring it to him, he says over and over again how grateful he is and what a good man I am. I go back into the warm house to cope with my guilt. I can never say that I had no room.

I am still looking into the kitchen cupboard, the carrier bag in my hand. I put into the carrier bag tins of soup, beans, and yes I suppose we can spare a tin of ham - just one - but not the salmon. It would be a waste to give it away, wouldn't it? I need my house, my lifestyle, my security. If I gave like you Lord, I'd have nothing left; it would be a living crucifixion.   I can pretend to identify with parishioners and the poor but all the time I keep enough back for my own comfort, my own security. When I give them tins of beans and money for the gas, I pretend it's what you would do Lord, but I know that you would give the salmon. You would eat the mouldy bread.

I pack the carrier bag. Half a loaf, some margarine, two eggs, a tin of beans and a packet of soup. Deborah is now warm. Her clothes are dry. She has money for heat and food for a day. I see her to the front door.   She walks out into the rainy winter night.   I dismiss her with a smile and words of encouragement. She walks down the path, steering Catherine in her pushchair under a winter night sky, pelting with rain. Through the gate and she is gone. I am relieved and feel that my obligation to her is now discharged. I do not say it, but in the back of my mind I am telling her not to bother me again. She gives me a bad conscience. I am glad to dismiss her.

When I utter the dismissal at the Eucharist, what do I mean? Do I mean, "Goodbye, my involvement with you is now finished. We have been so close, but I dare not share the bread of common experience?" Do I mean that from now our relationship is different? My duty to you my sister is now discharged? Go in peace.

2017 Postscript

It is January 2017. I have not been in ministry in Salford for over 20 years and I am retired, but I am passing through Salford on a bus. I see Robert (Chapter 1: Expectations) through the bus window. The first time I have seen him for many years. I go home, switch on my computer and find his address through 192.com. Some days later, I go to his home, unannounced. It is now on the 18th floor of a block of flats. I ring the bell. The door opens. For a moment, he looks at me, but then, as if there has been no passage of time, he says, "Hello Geoff. Come in."

The flat is sparsely furnished. There is a settee, one arm chair, one upright chair and a coffee table. There are no pictures on the wall. A small mat is the only floor covering, apart from a multitude of cigarette ends. He tells me that his parents are dead and his sister is in a home. Tea in a stained cup is on a coffee table in front of him. Robert rolls a cigarette and lights it. He offers me a cup of tea. "How are you, Geoff," he asks.

"Absolutely fine. How are you?"

"Terrible," he says. "I wish God would either show me his love or stop bothering me."

In the Eucharist, we declare ourselves to be the Body of Christ. God's instrument of love and power for good in the world is his Church - the Body of Christ. Robert has been waiting for intervention from the sky, but it is not God that has kept Robert waiting, but God's Body here on earth, his Church – I and all who break bread in His name. And for every Robert, there are countless others crying out for God's love, waiting, waiting for the love of God to be brought by you and me.

Other books by this author, available in paperback from Amazon and for Kindle

Weep Not For Me

In this powerful and moving book, Geoffrey Howard invites us to journey with him through the Stations of the Cross. The context is the inherent tension in trying to support both Jewish Communities in Salford, England and Palestinians in the West Bank. Bishop David Shepherd, in his Foreword writes, "This book offers us fresh insight into who Jesus is."

Wheelbarrow Across the Sahara

This is the account of Geoffrey Howard's 2,000 mile walk across the Sahara Desert in 1975. Humphrey Carpenter Writes, "This is the most extraordinary contemporary travel book I've ever read."

Chris Bonington writes, "Geoff Howard's sparkling humour makes this compulsive reading

Printed in Great Britain
by Amazon